EVANGELISM THAT WORKS!

A "HOW TO" MANUAL
ON
UNCONVENTIONAL SOUL WINNING

Huntington House Publishers

Huntington House Publishers
P.O. Box 53788
Lafayette, Louisiana 70505
Visit our website at
www.huntingtonhousebooks.com

Printed in the United States of America

Library of Congress
Card Catalog Number 00-108646
ISBN 1-56384-181-9

DEDICATION

To our Lord Jesus Christ for the revelation of His infinite love and compassion for people who are hurting in our world.

To Jannette, my dear wife, who always amazes me with her invariable attentiveness and support for my vision.

To Amy, Michelle, Michael, and Stevie, who bring refreshing diversion to my intense nature with their hugs and kisses.

To my loving, caring parents, Gerald and Beulah Derstine, whose faithful Christian example leaves a living legacy for my family.

To my sister Joanne, my secretary Ella LaMarre, and my friend Bob Armstrong, whose professional skills helped to make this book a reality.

To all my spiritual children, whose testimonies bring a constant source of inspiration and reward to my life.

To the spiritual fathers and mentors who have unselfishly contributed to my growth in knowledge and character.

To the courageous members of our church, people of vision, who have put into practice the principles of this book.

To my friends and ministry partners who support the vision with their prayers and financial gifts.

To all those who pray for me daily.

CONTENTS

v

FOREWORD

The book you are about to read concerns the foundational issue of our Christianity in relationship to the world at large—the winning of the lost. We are always enthused when an author's experience establishes the premise for his work. This book does not merely express ideas, it expounds on them. In a very practical manner, Pastor Phil Derstine develops passion for soul winning in the heart of the reader.

Yet, it is not merely inspiration that you, the reader, will obtain from these pages. In time-tested experiences, you will find good advice on becoming an effective witness in differing and creative situations.

It is exciting to think how this book will have an eternal impact on many lives. The many everyday examples of proven outreach methods are great "how-to's" when the "why to" becomes the "want to."

I especially appreciate the emphasis on reaching hurting people, as the Lord's heart is clearly for reaching all people, without forgetting the down and out.

I know that numerous people will be brought into the kingdom of God as this book challenges every reader to step outside their comfort zone and reach people in everyday settings right where they live.

Pastor Tommy Barnett

INTRODUCTION

This is the decade for *evangelism!* We hear it preached. We see a desperate hunger in people's hearts for spiritual things. The turn of the millennium brings new hope for change and innovative Last Days strategies to advance the Kingdom of God. We also know that the Bible promises a great ingathering of souls in the last days.

However, the obvious questions remain . . . *how, when,* and *where?* Perhaps we're waiting for someone to step forward with a plan, a new method, or formula. Maybe a revival will break out in some little church in "Nowheresville" and spread around the globe like wildfire, a sort of make-over of the 1950s Azusa Street.

Our current revival phenomena have challenged the church to repent and prepare for a mighty last day's harvest. We've been to the mountain. We've done our carpet time. Where is the *harvest?*

These questions have plagued me, and I've sought God much about the role of the Church in these last days. God has

11

given clear insight and instruction, which is the purpose of this writing.

For years, we have enjoyed a tremendous freedom of the Spirit in our local church. We've been revived. We've been renewed. And we've had a global vision, reaching out to thirty-eight nations of the world.

In more recent years, God has been challenging us in some deliberate local evangelism efforts: to literally obey the commands of Christ and take the Gospel to our city; to respond to the words of Acts 1:8 and take our witness to Jerusalem and to all Judea; to deliberately "unlearn" some of the traditional methods that seem to lack effectiveness anyway, and attempt to be led by the Spirit of God.

The world is changing. People are changing. Even though the Gospel remains the same, we have to follow the Spirit's lead in administering this life-changing Gospel, showing its relevance to people today and allowing Christ to touch the needs of today. We need a new wineskin for this new wine.

The Gospel works best in crisis.

People today are in crisis.

More and more people are becoming

disillusioned with traditional "church religion." They're searching for spirituality in other ways. They're looking for help in their problems.

The world offers solutions to problems in ways that it understands. Science invents new drugs and psychologists, new theories and methods of counseling or psychoanalyzing. Much time is given to defining the problems.

People are experimenting with their own solutions, some of which are against the laws of our land . . . illegal drugs, illicit sex, or physical violence and abuse.

The challenge for the church in the next decade is to show the relevance of the Gospel of Jesus Christ to effectively meet the needs of people right where they are, to take Christ to the people. The Church must take Christ from the comfort and convenience of our church buildings out to the streets or wherever the people are.

We understand clearly that salvation is given to *all* men. God doesn't save us because we're *righteous* or because we're *whole*, but rather, He saves us to *make us* righteous and to *make us* whole.

Therefore, the Gospel begins right at the point of need and carries with it all the ingredients and potential to help, to heal, and to correct the crisis that people are in. The Gospel of Jesus Christ has supernatural, life-changing *power!*

But the Gospel must be *heard.*

The Apostle Paul asks in Romans 10:14, "How then shall they call on him in whom they have not believed? And how shall they believe in him of whom they have not HEARD? And how shall they HEAR without a preacher?"

The life-changing power of the Gospel has absolutely no chance to work if the message is not *heard* and *received* by those who are in need. No matter how valuable the medicine, it has no chance to work unless it is properly administered.

Do we really believe that our Gospel message carries inherent power that can help people with real problems? Then we must get serious about effectively administering it, so that it will be readily received.

In the pages that follow, I hope to inspire *you* to action. In a simple and conversational way, I want to introduce you to a fresh evangelism philosophy for these Last Days, along with illustrations of how it is working in our local church and city.

I don't want to be so presumptuous as to suggest that everything that is working for us will work the same for you, but the biblical principles are clear. God has given the revelation and has allowed us to prove it in our own testing ground. A pattern and model has emerged that can be applied in a variety of ways in other places.

The redundancy of certain phrases and ideas advanced throughout this writing is intentional. You must get this message into your spirit.

Allow the principles and illustrations advanced in this book to inspire your creativity, draw upon the Spirit of God, and take you to your knees. God has a unique plan for your life and your church. His divine destiny is upon you.

It is powerful. It is supernatural. Experience it and enter the joy of an unconventional soul winning Last Day's harvest!

1.

BREAKING OUT OF YOUR COMFORT ZONE

Thick with cigarette smoke, the darkened room thumped to a rock'n'roll beat and reeked of cheap liquor and stale perfume. I pushed up to the bar. My mind wandered to the warmth and comfort of my home and family only minutes away.

"What am I doing here?" I asked myself. Picturing someone of my sheltered past ministering in a barroom to the dark recesses of society brought a wry smile to my face.

Only days ago, standing at the helm of my pastorate, I had delivered a well-organized sermon to a well-adjusted congregation of well-dressed people. Tonight the bar was my pulpit, the bruised and broken my congregation, and the open streets my church.

It began three years earlier, when I agreed one night to ride along in an unmarked squad car with a sheriff's deputy, a member of our church.

"Come with me for a look at our city after dark," he insisted. "It will open your eyes."

We walked the aisles of adult bookstores and peep shows. We witnessed the activity of prostitutes and drug dealers in the shadowy underworld of fear and mistrust.

I was shocked. We weren't on the streets of Chicago, New York, or Los Angeles. This was Bradenton—a sleepy little retirement town on the central west coast of Florida. This wasn't supposed to be happening in my town!

God planted something fresh in my heart that night. The image of hurting, captive people drove me to His Word, seeking biblical guidelines for reaching this dark corner of hurting society, largely ignored by the church.

Shaking Tradition

A closer look at the Gospels and the Acts of the Apostles shook my traditional views of soul winning.

There were no altar calls, no show of hands, no sinner's prayers. "How did they get anyone saved?" I asked myself.

Traditional evangelism makes soul winning burdensome, unnatural, and largely ineffective. With altar calls, sinner's prayers, a "show of hands," the Four Spiritual Laws, the Roman's Road . . . all this methodology thrusts the task of winning souls into the professional arena and out of reach for most Christians. Jesus didn't teach or practice these methods.

At this time, God gave me a clear instruction. "Take My presence out of the church building and into the dark corners of your community. Take the power of My Word closer to the problems. Just go! I will make the appointments. I will provide opportunities."

The words were a command. Fresh ideas followed.

A friend joined me in walking the streets of our city at night, moving among the people, and learning the lay of the land. Being raised in a devout Christian home with a strong Mennonite tradition didn't make it easy for me to do this. I felt like a fish out of water. At times I wondered if I was endangering my heart with all I was seeing.

In the words of Jeremiah, "Mine eye

affected mine heart" (Lam. 3:51). I knew
I was being changed by what I was seeing.
For the first time in my life, I was receiv-
ing a burden for the lost. I was hearing
the groaning of the prisoner, like David in
Psalms 102:20.

We felt like spies in the Promised Land,
sent ahead to look over Canaan. God made
it clear that we were not to throw the gospel at people. We were to move with compassion toward people as Jesus did (Mark
6:34) and to be slow to speak and quick to
listen, allowing the Holy Spirit to do the
work.

A couple of months went by without a
single conversion. Although our efforts
seemed fruitless, we still felt fulfillment in
simply obeying God's command to go. God
was doing something in our hearts. He
was breaking down our own plans and
building our confidence in Him.

Then, as if heaven's floodgates were
opened all at once, the Spirit of God began scheduling divine appointments.
Night after night, we encountered Spirit
orchestrated opportunities for dynamic
ministry.

One early and unforgettable episode
took place in a barroom. That night we
walked into a tavern and sat down at the

corner of the bar. We sipped coffee and waited to see what God would do.

On the stool near me was a young woman dressed in faded blue jeans, her long, sandy hair in disarray. She was nervous and jittery, drinking beer, face down, and minding her own business. Suddenly she burst into tears.

"Are you okay?" I turned and asked tentatively.

"Yes . . . well NO, not really," she replied.

Fighting the urge to jump in at the first sign of opportunity, I obeyed the Spirit and waited. The girl regained her composure and then minutes later lost it again. This time she turned toward me.

Through her sobbing, she unraveled the twisted story of her pain. She shared how she had gone from a broken home to a life of prostitution on the streets, fueled by a debilitating cocaine addiction.

I listened. She told me how she had been living with an older man, trading sexual favors for money to support her drug habit. Disgusted with herself, she recently broke away from the relationship, only to find herself out on the streets in even more desperate and demeaning circumstances.

She wept openly, a common occurrence in a barroom . . . it doesn't seem to bother others. Her story continued and often she interjected, "I don't know why I'm telling you all this."

In my spirit, I knew.

Suddenly she blurted, "I had a dream recently, and I think it was from God!"

Now we're getting somewhere, I thought, musing in my spirit how God was setting this all up.

She told me the dream, which, to my amazement was actually being fulfilled right there in the bar, with our meeting and conversation. I waited for the prompting of the Holy Spirit and then broke the silence.

"Cindy," I said, "Your dream was from God! And I'm the man of God that was sent to bring you the Light. You see, I'm a minister, and today is the day of Salvation for you!"

She exploded into tears. Tears of joy. "I knew there was something different about you," she exclaimed. "Now I know what I must do."

I followed her out to her car in the parking lot where she retrieved her stash of drugs and paraphernalia, handing it to me, relieved and in tears. With the drugs in one hand and my other hand on her shoulder, we prayed to God as we stood beside her car. This broken young woman found her peace in the outstretched arms of Jesus. It was the day of her salvation!

We went back into the bar to telephone her parents who lived in Michigan. To my surprise, they were spirit-filled believers who had been praying for years that their wayward daughter would be found.

Next, I called Jannette, my wife. By this time it was after midnight. "I have to bring this one home," I said apologetically.

In a rare and rewarding swirl of activity, we took Cindy off the streets and flew her home to her family and a good, spirit-filled church . . . the next day . . . all within twenty-four hours.

Incredible? No.

Unconventional? Perhaps.

Supernatural? Absolutely!

I believe God is directing the church today into supernatural, soul winning directions.

That's evangelism with less emphasis on methods and more emphasis on the

Spirit's leading. The secret to supernatural soul winning is sharing the good news "not with persuasive words of human wisdom, but in demonstration of the Spirit of power" (I Cor. 2:4, NKJV).

Unconventional Soul Winning

I write, then, to unmask a rather simple and natural act for a healthy Christian . . . soul winning. The very word strikes paralyzing fear in the hearts of comfortable Christians today. We've become heavenly minded but no earthly good, interested in heavenly bliss but not our earthly assignment, aware of the command but unwilling to commit.

My purpose in writing is to advance a model of soul winning that will release the Body of Christ to do what God has already uniquely equipped her to do . . . win the lost to Jesus Christ, to take the fear out of soul winning; to make it fun, to link you up to the Holy Spirit's ability to minister through you in these critical Last Days.

I call it unconventional soul winning. Is it like "Friendship Evangelism"? Or, "Power Evangelism"? How about "Relationship Evangelism"?

To all these questions I answer "Yes" and I answer "No." The difference in this Holy Spirit approach is the focus on your unique gifts and calling and God's divine participation in your efforts.

Realizing our insufficiency and God's totality (II Cor. 3:5,6) we become more able by depending fully upon Him. Unconventional soul winning, therefore, is more about being . . . being who you are, being at the right place at the right time, being willing, being bold, being natural, and being completely sold!

Your interest in reading this book is proof positive of your desire to obey God's command to win souls. The principles and concepts of soul winning outlined herein are both simple and profound, simple to understand and profoundly effective if applied. It's my prayer that pastors will take the lead in applying these principles and that cities will be turned right side up!

Soul winning is one of the most misunderstood subjects in the Bible. What God intended to be simple, fun, and natural in the process of reproducing healthy believers, theologians have made an abstract system of ways and means. Most have adopted a programmatic form of witnessing, passed down through a dead institution.

Read this book carefully and thoughtfully. Don't speed read or rush through. Neither try to memorize or outline the principles. Simply digest it prayerfully and get it into your spirit. If you understand what you are reading and let it find place in your heart, then the Holy Spirit will bring it back to your attention at precisely the right moment to apply it to any given situation.

For too long, the Body of Christ has shirked the responsibility of proclaiming the Gospel in a relevant way. It's time for Christians to understand their God-given task to change the world. It's time for Christians to understand how God has uniquely equipped them for the task.

It's time for unconventional soul winning.

2.

WAKE UP, CHURCH!

For God to do what He desires to do in America, the Church is going to have to get honest. The arrogance and self-righteousness must stop. The mistaken priorities and competition must stop. The internal politics and carnal agendas must give way to a genuine interest in the heart and plan of God.

God will not share His glory. God will not display His miraculous amidst so much counterfeit. As long as the Church is satisfied with cheap imitations, she will not experience the true revival and harvest for which she longs.

The greatest challenge for the Church in this important hour will be to discard traditional and largely ineffective ways of doing things in favor of true ministry by the Spirit, evidenced by fruit that remains.

Never before have we been so plagued by shortsighted, short order, programmatic forms of worship and evangelism choked in a mire of pride and self-aggrandizement.

Years of prosperity have made the American church self-centered and ingrown. Instead of investing in the Kingdom of God and His plan and purposes, we have invested in ourselves, our plans and our purposes. The result is a spiritually anemic Church, hidden within the four walls of our comfortable meetinghouses. We celebrate with *hocus pocus* spiritualism that entertains the saints but is largely ignored by the world as irrelevant or ridiculous.

The Church today is accepted by the saints and ignored by the world. The ministry of Jesus was just the opposite . . . He captured the world's attention while religion tried to block Him out. Whatever revival the church is experiencing today is mostly ingrown and ignored by the world. True revival cannot be contained and will not be ignored.

Obedience

The only answer and saving grace for

the Church is obedience to the call and heart of God. In two words . . . soul winning. It's the only reason we are still here awaiting our Lord's return. "And this Gospel of the kingdom shall be preached in all the world: for a witness unto all nations; and then shall the end come" (Matt. 24:14).

While the Bible repeatedly warns us of a last days "form of Godliness . . . denying the power thereof" and the "itching ears . . . ever learning. . . . heaping unto ourselves teachers," life goes on as usual in most churches in America. Even in Spirit-filled churches . . . the same routine of praise, preaching, and programs.

Our excellent presentations lack sincerity to the point of alienating the very world that they are intended to reach. Christ's message of Good News, saving grace, unconditional love, forgiveness, and deliverance is shrouded by a dark cloud of condemnation, doctrinal debate, and Hollywood professionalism.

"Wake-up, Church, and smell the roses!"

The harvest is still plentiful and the working laborers are few. Never before in the history of the American Church has there been such a spiritual hunger and recognition of need in our nation. The search for answers is on. The world is crying out.

Psychics and godless cults are on the rise. Young people are trying to find identity through sex, drugs, and gang participation. Even Hollywood producers have posed the questions through movies like "Leap of Faith" and "Sister Act." Prime-time television shows "Seventh Heaven" and "Touched By An Angel" reveal the world's search for spiritual reality.

Where is the Church? Where are the people of God who will passionately carry God's saving grace to an apostate generation? Perhaps they are busy planning the next church social or putting the final touches on this year's Christmas program.

It's time for the Church to "redress" herself, repackage the "old-time religion" and take it to the streets where the people are. Discard the ritualistic, programmatic forms of the past and enter the real world with all its horrendous imperfections.

Ministry is messy. Always has been, always will be. No guts, no Glory! Jesus was criticized by the religious people of His day for moving out among the sinners . . . which is exactly where the church should be.

Racing for Jesus

Our church has entered the racing arena. Auto racing is the largest spectator sport in the nation and as a weekend event it caters to the unchurched, a good fishing hole to say the least. With the purchase of a Junior Dragster for our Youth Department and the sponsoring of a drag motorcycle, and late-model stock car, owned and driven by church members, we enjoy a high profile at the track.

"Racing for Jesus" brightly adorns the bodies of these rolling billboards and opportunities abound for one-on-one witnessing by our "Racing Team" of soul winners. We pass out "Daily Race Record" cards, custom made tracts with utility value that share the gospel and provide space for race fans to record the results of their favorite cars.

With the blessing of racetrack operators, we provide a team of official chaplains for national events. Organizers of these huge thirty to forty-thousand people gatherings have recognized the need for spiritual help teams to be dispatched along with medical and security teams—radio dispatched to minister prayer to people in crisis situations!

Our evangelism agenda has changed from an attempt to notch our guns with short-order conversions to that of occupying enemy territory and taking dominion through a demonstration of God's love. Praying for people's needs often precedes the presentation of salvation's plan. One-on-one ministry is labor intensive with little glitz and glamour, but as Jesus himself demonstrated, meeting needs makes disciples rather than converts and produces fruit that remains.

Hell House

Over the Halloween season, our Youth Department advances an evangelistic counterpart to the traditional haunted house. It is called Hell House and is celebrated as the scariest exhibit on the West Coast of Florida. Thousands of teen-agers wait hours in line to hear the Gospel presented in shocking reality and living color.

In a live dramatization of the evil spirit world that lurks behind the lifestyles of drug and alcohol addiction, "safe sex," abortion, suicide, and more, youth are challenged to choose Christ, the giver of Life.

Over the years, our counselors have recorded hundreds of first-time salvations and thousands have received prayer and follow-up. Our success with this unique ministry idea has been reported on ABC, NBC, CBS, and CNN.

In the coming years, pastors must teach their congregations how to occupy the community, the school system, the marketplace, the media, and the political machine. This must occur, not for the purpose of enacting the right laws and administrative procedures, but for the purpose of radiating the presence of God, imparting the power of the Holy Spirit, and ministering the saving grace of Jesus Christ.

The Church must get a vision for changing the world from the inside out. One cannot legislate morality and Christian ethics. Only a heart change will bring any lasting change. Only a heart change will have redemptive value. Laws and cultural practice will follow the heart and character change of a civilization. Isn't this what Jesus meant by ministering the Kingdom of God?

Coffee House

We opened a coffee house for the homeless in our inner city, offering job search, showers, lockers, and laundry services. Politicians and local clergy were skeptical of our intentions as we cloaked an old-fashioned discipleship program with modern mentoring vernacular.

The glaring success of our efforts, however, drew such favor that the city advanced forty thousand dollars to fund an innovative program that pays churches to adopt a homeless person or family. In an innovative blend of church and state, our city applied tax dollars to the compassionate arm of the local church . . . and some said it couldn't be done.

I believe this is just the beginning. As the world's problems grow beyond man's abilities to solve them, people and governments will look for help from above. Herein lies the opportunity for the Church. Herein lies the seedbed for a great revival in America.

Wake-up, Church, and minister the way Jesus did . . . meeting the needs of people, both tangible and spiritual. Study your community to discover what and where the needs really are. Meet the needs that people are aware of and then introduce people to the permanent solution they may not be aware of . . . faith in Jesus Christ unto salvation!

Instead of glossy tracts and slick marketing campaigns, allow your life to be a "living epistle, read of all men." Let the church assembly become a huddle where the team gets its marching orders for the real game that's played out in the highways and hedges of life.

Today *is* the day of salvation. As the world system gets darker and more hopeless in the natural, the hunger for a spiritual solution becomes more intense, more desperate. There is a vacuum drawing the Church out to the real needs of society. There is an emptiness that only God can fill.

Wake-up, Church! Enter this new millennium with a renewed sense of purpose. Be willing to break tradition. Be willing to change. Be willing to embrace the heart of God for the souls of mankind.

God's Highest Priority

Soul winning is God's highest priority. God has a plan for planet earth. It is a plan that involves redeeming a lost and sinful people back into right standing with God, redeeming souls from the death that the original sins of Adam and Eve have brought and winning souls in the proverbial game of life, a timeless struggle between good and evil.

The time curve on our world's very existence is shaped by the advancement of soul winning. God has a plan to redeem mankind. He is not willing that any should perish, but that all would come to repentance. He is patient concerning His promise of salvation. "The Lord is not slack concerning his promise, as some men count slackness; but is long-suffering to us-ward, not willing that any should perish, but that all should come to repentance" (II Pet. 3:9).

Yet, we know that not all will come to repentance. A place of everlasting torment is prepared for the rebellious who will hear but not receive the Lord's gift of salvation.

It would seem in error that God's plan to redeem mankind would require the use of mankind to do the job. While people are the problem, God still intends to use people to administer the solution. We are a lost people, yet we are appointed to carry out His plan of salvation.

1. Every Christian is commanded to be a soul winner.
2. There must be a great harvest of souls before the Lord's return.
3. Man's methods and programs have failed.
4. Traditional methods of sharing Christ are largely ineffective in today's modern culture.
5. God is revealing new and innovative ways to reach this generation with the Gospel.
6. Great joy comes to those who are obedient to the Lord's command to win souls.
7. God has uniquely equipped His people for the task.

The last words of Jesus in Mark 16:15 instruct us to go into the entire world and preach the gospel to every creature. He emphasized the priority of this assignment by making it His final instruction. He never instructed us to busy ourselves with building the church. In fact, He stated, "I will build my church . . ." (Matt. 16:18).

Jesus died for the world, not the church. He says in Luke 15:7, "I say unto you, that likewise joy shall be in heaven over one sinner that repenteth, more than over ninety and nine just persons, which need no repentance."

Matthew 24:14, He reminds us, "And this gospel of the Kingdom shall be preached in all the world for a witness unto all nations; and then shall the end come." It's as if God is patiently waiting for the church to grow up in the understanding of our purpose for being and engage the task of soul winning, and finish the job, and then He will return!

K.I.S.S.

"Keep It Simple, Sweetheart." The late Dr. Harold Hill was a beloved Christian lecturer of the seventies who frequented Christian Retreat. I was drawn to him because, despite his exhaustive educational background, he had an ability to cut through the academics and relate truth to the common man. Referring to his esteemed colleagues as "egg heads," he bemoaned our tendencies toward over-complicating simple truths of life. A result of too much information in a world dominated by the "boob tube," or "one-eyed monster," a couple of the names he gave for modern-day television. "Keep it simple,

sweetheart," he used to say (a slight modi-
fication of the term used in the secular
world).

Underscoring the command of Christ,
to "Go ye," we must simplify our soul winning programs. "Everyone a soul winner"
must be our motto. As a squirrel is to nuts,
so is a Christian to winning souls . . .
uniquely equipped by God to go out and
hunt "lost nuts." Only too often, we find
the squirrels busy scrabbling around the
bird feeder. The traditional church has
become a comfortable feeding ground and
has lost sight of her true calling.

Complex how-to programs of scripture
memorization and evangelism apologetics
only serve to mystify and alienate the av-
erage Christian. Never feeling quite up to
the task, most Christians live silent lives,
largely insulated from the world they are
supposed to reach.

Our silent witness or godly lifestyle,
alone, will not win a soul to Christ. Romans 10:14 tells us that the Gospel must
be spoken. We're each responsible to speak
to those in our circle of influence.

Taking the fear and mystique out of
soul winning is the only way to mobilize
the Church into the mighty last day's har-

vest. Recognizing our own insufficiency, we must teach total dependency upon the Holy Spirit (II Cor. 3:5, 6).

Luke 21:15 promises that God will help us speak. "For I will give you a mouth and wisdom, which all your adversaries shall not be able to gainsay nor resist." They won't be able to mock or resist you . . . or should I say, the Holy Spirit within you!

Seven Steps—The Jesus Way

This seven-step approach is at the heart of our unconventional soul winning strategy. It's the Jesus way of one-on-one witnessing.

1. Smile

Seems simple enough. Yet some Christians need to get in front of a mirror and practice! A smile creates a friendly atmosphere, one of kindness and acceptance. Many people today come from dysfunctional homes, and they struggle with rejection. God helps the church to be a functional family with a friendly disposition.

One night as I sat in a bar waiting for God's direction as to who to talk to, the bartender commented on my smile. "You have the warmest smile," she commented inquisitively. A conversation ensued, revealing her plans to have an abortion due to an unexpected pregnancy. "I'm 40-years-old, I've already raised my children, I don't need any more," she said. "Besides, I don't want to marry the guy anyway."

I smiled and commented that the baby would look just like her. "It's not a baby," she responded, "Just a fetus!" Nevertheless, my comment touched a sensitive nerve, and she was troubled.

A couple more visits to that bar brought further conversation on the matter. She discovered that I was a minister, and I had opportunity to pray with her. One day she changed her plans and decided against abortion. To this day, whenever I go into that bar, she shows me the most recent photos of her son and introduces me as the pastor responsible for her having the child. (Sometimes that needs further explanation!) A smile . . . can save a mother and child.

2. Engage Conversation

A smile can open the door for friendly conversation. But you must *engage* conversation. You must *initiate* it. Learn to take an interest in people. Jesus moved toward people (Matt. 14:14, Mark 6:34), and so must we. Trust God to give you the words to speak. It's really not as difficult as we try to make it.

My partner and I were ministering to a young man in the parking lot of a bar, and a biker watched from his bike nearby. He didn't look friendly or interested, but I knew we would have to talk to him next because he was parked right in our path. Leaning back on the raised seat of his Harley, arms crossed and boots propped up on the handlebars, he seemed to be daring us to speak to him.

As we approached, my mind was screaming, "What am I going to say?" Each step brought me closer to the reality that I was blank; I simply didn't know what to say. We arrived, and I blurted, "Hi." (That wasn't so hard.)

He responded, "I was hoping you'd come talk with me."

We discovered, to my surprise, that he was the son of a preacher. He was running from the call of God on his life and disgusted with religion. Yet, he was most impressed to see church people out on the streets ministering. We prayed with him, planting a seed for his salvation.

Luke 21:13-15 says, "And it [they] shall turn to you for a testimony. Settle it therefore in your hearts, not to meditate before what ye shall answer. For I will give you a mouth and wisdom, which all your adversaries shall not be able to gainsay nor resist."

3. Discover Their Need

Engage conversation for the purpose of discovering their need. You don't have to talk to anyone very long before they will complain about something. That is their need. Their need creates an opportunity for you to offer prayer.

I remember late one night when my partner and I were walking down 14th Street, the strip in our inner city. We met a young man of lean, muscular build walking toward us. I greeted him with a "What's happening?" in an attempt to start some conversation. Startled, he jumped back into a fighting stance . . . he was angry and wanted to fight. Loudly and with foul language, he expressed his violent intentions, his arms flailing around in front of our faces.

We stood motionless, a little surprised, but without fear, waiting for him to take a breath so that we could get a word in

edgewise. When he did, I heard my partner say, "What would you say if I told you
that I loved you?"

My mind said, "Oh no . . . now he'll
think we're gay. . . now we're really dead!"

But to my surprise, he melted. "I'd say,
I like that!" he responded gingerly. Then
he began telling us that his father was
passed out in a cheap hotel room down
the street, and they didn't have a friend in
town. He was on his way to find a woman
and a bottle, then drink himself to sleep.
Both he and his father were out of work
and at the end of their rope.

We had the opportunity to lead that
young man to Christ that night, and when
he repeated the prayer with us, he did it
with all his might, in the same loud voice
he had attacked us with earlier. Despite
the jeers and heckles of people passing by,
he prayed loudly and fearlessly, with the
kind of sincerity rarely seen in the church
building today.

We had engaged conversation and discovered his need for the purpose of offering prayer, and God did the rest!

4. Offer Prayer

Consider prayer to be your highest
order of spiritual business, rather than

making a convert. Prayer engages God, and you can't expect to lead someone to the Lord without God's help anyway.

For too long, we have applied clever debate tactics or marketing strategies to coax people into repeating a sinner's prayer. Jesus said in John 6:44, "No man can come to me, except the Father which has sent me draw him . . ." We must get God involved in our witnessing opportunities as soon as possible. This is comfortably done by offering prayer.

Now, you must learn how to offer prayer confidently. Do not ask people if you can pray for them. They may not know what that means, "Will I have to get down on my knees? . . . or come see your priest?" No, you must assume that they will value prayer for their need, and most do. After all, if you're offering prayer, then you must have a better connection to God than they do! What do they have to lose?

Most people have an inherent respect for two things: the Holy Bible and prayer. They may not be the least bit interested in what church you attend or the doctrine you follow, but they value prayer.

Let me teach you how to offer prayer. Try this simple phrase: "Before I leave, I'd like to pray with you about that matter (name it) . . . here, just take my hand."

Then place your right hand in theirs, as if you are shaking hands, and place your other hand on top. In this way you are placing both hands upon them in a non-confrontational way, but literally fulfilling Mark 16:18, ". . . they shall lay hands on the sick and they shall recover."

Pray a short prayer. Expect the windows of heaven to open when you pray. You are linking them up with God! I like to imagine a powerful beam of light from heaven surrounding us at that time of prayer and the angels descending and ascending. Allow God to intervene by His Spirit. Believe that He is doing the work!

"Therefore I say unto you, What things soever ye desire, when you pray, believe that ye receive them, and ye shall have them" (Mark 11:24).

My children know that I often orchestrate a prayer opportunity with the waitress or waiter at the restaurants at which we eat. After they bring our food, it's customary for the waiter to ask, "Is there any thing else I can do for you [before I leave to wait on others]?" To which I say, "Yes, you can join us for prayer over the food," and I reach for their hand as our family is joining hands. They accommodate; after all, I am the customer, right?

I pray a prayer over the food and a blessing upon our waiter. This often spawns further conversation and prayer. It's fun and effective. And it's very natural, not pushy or uncomfortable.

5. Use Discernment

After prayer, pause briefly to observe what God is doing. You may see tears streaming down their faces . . . it doesn't take a lot of discernment here to know that God is doing something. They may ask you to pray with them about something else. Perhaps nothing may be apparent to your understanding. This is where you must listen to the Spirit of God for the next step. You may have simply sown some seed, and your witness ends here, or God may work through you to bring in the harvest. You will learn to use your spiritual discernment simply through experience. Believe me, when you get this far, God will not let you down!

6. Introduce Christ

Now that you have their attention and you have earned the right to take them further, move them beyond their needs and into God's gift of salvation.

Ask them if they would like you to pray a prayer to give them an assurance of salvation. Ask them if they know about God sending His son, Jesus, to die on a cross for the sins of mankind. Speak about God's promise of eternal life and heaven's reward over Hell's fury.

Lead them through a believer's prayer. Just spontaneously compose a prayer that follows the order of Romans 10:9-10: "If thou shalt confess with thy mouth the Lord Jesus, and shalt believe in thine heart that God hath raised him from the dead, thou shalt be saved. For with the heart man believeth unto righteousness; and with the mouth confession is made unto salvation."

A simple tool to remember is the *ABC*s of Salvation:

A-Admit you are a sinner
B-Believe in your heart that Christ
    rose from the dead
C-Confess with your mouth the Lord-
    ship of Jesus.

7. Make an Appointment

Finally, make an appointment. Don't ever lead someone to the Lord without letting them know when they will see you again. In fact, make an appointment to meet them at church next Sunday, or better yet, pick them up for church next Sunday.

Whenever you sow the seed of Salvation into the heart of a new believer, the enemy will try to immediately steal it away. Fears and doubts can cause someone to question and discount what God has done. Knowing that they will see you again soon will cause them to hold on.

Remember, God didn't call us to make converts, but rather, disciples. Discipling will require more of your time, more of your life. We've found that the strategies of unconventional soul winning work for everyone, young or old, and in a variety of real world situations. On the streets, door-to-door, in parks, in bars, in jails, in nursing homes, hospitals, shopping malls, racetracks, flea markets, and truck-stops . . . wherever there are people. We celebrate on-the-job training over classroom academics and give testimony time center stage in our services.

Creativity and uniqueness is the key to multiplication. We pray for the Holy Spirit to give fresh ideas that will capture the

imagination of the people and the interest of the secular world. A simple but fresh
idea can take your city by storm.

Take It to the Streets

In 1987, on the heels of the nation-
ally publicized PTL scandal, our church
experienced some division and financial
problems. I was devastated. A year earlier,
I had accepted the appointment by the
elders as senior pastor, a decision that
didn't come easy for me.

Growing up in the vocation with parents in full-time ministry allowed me to
understand the demands and sacrifices it
required. I didn't know for sure what I
wanted to be "when I grew up," but I was
certain of one thing . . . I never wanted to
be a preacher!

I didn't want the responsibility of being "good" all the time. I didn't want to
wear the label of "preacher," or "rever-
end." Most of all, I didn't want to live in
the fishbowl of public scrutiny that so often plagued the lives of my parents. All
that reasoning melted away one day, however, when God manifested Himself to me
in a personal way, through a series of
dreams and visions. But more on that later.

Just a year into my pastorate, our church was faced with division in our Christian Retreat community. I remember going on a routine missionary trip to Honduras during that time and experiencing great revival services. Hundreds of people were saved and healed. My spirit was renewed.

On the plane trip home, I felt the heaviness beginning to return. I didn't want to return home to my church. I didn't want to face the strife and confusion that I knew awaited me. I'll never forget that moment, on a commercial airline, passing over Cuba. I was looking out the window, through an exceptionally clear sky, noting the markings on the ground below that indicated the corridor of air space through which planes were safe to pass over the nation of Cuba.

It was here that I heard God speak. "Take it to the streets." The words were clear and bold, almost audible to my natural ears. Before I had time to question the command, it came again. "Take my Word to the streets of your city."

A rush flooded over my spirit as I knew I had heard from God. Yet I didn't know what it really meant. I didn't know how to obey or where to begin.

Not until the police officer in my church offered to show me the streets of our city at night, "when good people like you are in bed sleeping." Those were his words. They came just weeks after God had spoken to my heart on that airplane. God was divinely ordering my steps.

Actually our church is located in the suburbs, some fifteen miles out of the inner city. I was never raised in the city. Neither was I raised in the world. My virgin eyes were opened when I saw the darkness and perversion. My heart was grieved to think that somehow our message of deliverance was hidden behind the four walls of our comfortable church building.

The city streets of America are a heart-wrenching mission field. With drugs, alcohol, prostitution and homelessness on the increase, there is a desperate cry for help. The world is running out of answers. This is an hour of opportunity for the church to bring a supernatural solution . . . Jesus is the answer!

Together with a partner, I started walking our city streets one night each week. For me it was more than ministry. It was therapeutic. First-hand experiences with people in desperate need brought passion into my preaching and illustrations galore. The Word was being preached and God thrust our local church out onto the city streets like never before. We started in small ways.

1) **Feeding the hungry**—On 9 June, I preached a message about miracles, from Mark 6, the story of Jesus feeding the five thousand. Illustrating the message, I broke five loaves (hot-dog buns) and the elders distributed them to the entire congregation. It was miracle enough that everyone received a piece of bread. But some wondered if we'd have twelve baskets left over (Mark 6:43).

Surprisingly, this service marked the beginning of an extraordinary source of bread for our food closet, and we began delivering bread by the truckload, door-to-door, in needy parts of our city.

On 4 July, we began taking dinner to the homeless once a week, outdoors, at a public park in our city, feeding from thirty to seventy-five people each week.

2) **Clothes for the needy**—Our clothes closet began to explode as well. Donations of good used clothing began coming in from unexpected sources, and more fami-

lies began requesting the aid.

We have found feeding and clothing the needy a most rewarding ministry, one that directly fulfills Matthew 25:35, 36. Then Jesus says in verse 40, "Inasmuch as ye have done it unto one of the least of these my brethren, ye have done it unto me."

3) **Outdoor meetings**—We had been conducting outdoor meetings in needy parts of town for several years, mostly as an offshoot of our bus ministry. In 1991 we began to recognize this type of ministry as an effective soul winning tool. We serve a meal, perform music, drama, dance, and even circus acts to draw the crowd. Afterward, we boldly proclaim the Gospel through various testimonies and the preaching of the Word. Altar calls at these outdoor crusades yield hundreds of souls saved and lives changed.

4) **Door-to-door ministry**—We began touching our local community through door-to-door ministry, praying for the needs of people as the primary goal. We've had the glorious opportunity to pray for hundreds through these efforts.

5) **Fourteenth Street Coffee House**— Our boldest endeavor was the introduc-

tion of a storefront mission on the notori-
ously needy street of our city... Fourteenth
Street. We had to go through a vigorous
approval process with City Hall for this
facility to open. Here we distributed food
and clothing by day and counseled street
people at night, offering free coffee,
doughnuts, and prayer, seven days a week.
Our primary objective was to present the
Gospel and to assist people in securing
jobs.

Our efforts on the streets are more than
a passing fancy. God has planted a love
for this kind of ministry deep into my
heart. For three years I took the lead, witnessing on the streets weekly, praying with
people in the bars, and helping some out
of drug or alcohol addictions. Then, God
began raising up others in the church.

Pastor Tommy Barnett of Phoenix First
Assembly practices and teaches these principles, mobilizing a mega-church in Phoenix, Arizona, with over two hundred outreach ministries. Then at retirement age,
Brother Tommy launched another great
outreach church in California, the L.A. International Church, affectionately known
as the Dream Center, with son, Matthew
Barnett at the helm. These churches are

effectively teaching the Biblical principles of equipping every believer to be an able minister and compassionately modeling the ministry of Christ.

Today our street ministry flourishes, facilitated by people saved off the street, trained to minister, and now returning to help others. These redeemed, recycled converts are living testimonies of the delivering power of God. They are more effective in street ministry than I could ever be. I'm proud of them and thankful to God for what He has done.

3.

UNCONVENTIONAL SOUL WINNING

Mark 16:15 says, "Go ye into all the world and preach the gospel to every creature." We know that we are called of God to take the Gospel to all of creation.

The Gospel of Jesus Christ is not religious practice. Rather, it is a relationship with God, through the Holy Spirit. Religion will never satisfy. Man has a need to discover relationship with his creator.

How do we effectively introduce man to God? How do we preach the Gospel and bring others to the knowledge of Christ?

Jesus didn't teach or practice our familiar methods. So what example did He leave for us to follow? A review of His simple ministry style reveals the principles of what I call unconventional soul winning.

Principle 1—Meet People at the Point of Their Need

The Bible says that Jesus went about "doing good." Acts 10:38, "How God anointed Jesus of Nazareth with the Holy Ghost and with power: who went about doing good, and healing all that were oppressed of the devil; for God was with him."

Doing well under the leadership and unction of the Holy Spirit . . . it's a powerful combination. Jesus met people at the point of their need. To the sick, He was a healer. To the lonely, He was a friend. He became an advocate for the woman caught in adultery. He fed the hungry and provided for the poor.

In Luke 4, He introduced His ministry by reading these words from Isaiah the prophet (Isa. 61:1-2).

Luke 4:18, "The Spirit of the Lord is upon me, because he hath anointed me to preach the gospel to the poor; he hath sent me to heal the brokenhearted, to preach deliverance to the captives, and recovering of sight to the blind, to set at liberty them that are bruised."

Jesus went about relating to people and looking for needs. Christ becomes relevant at the point of need, because He brings answers to questions and solutions to problems.

Jesus never tried to convert people. He simply went around meeting the needs of people, and then they wanted to follow Him. As they followed, He was able to make them disciples.

Matthew 28:19 says, "Go ye therefore and teach all nations, baptizing them in the name of the Father, and of the Son, and of the Holy Ghost."

The word "teach" in the Greek is *matheteuo,* meaning to enroll as a pupil . . . to disciple. By command and by example, Jesus instructs us to go and make disciples.

Our short order, cookie-cutter, conversion tactics often alienate people. Nobody likes to be sold something that they don't know they need. However, people will drive all over town to find the place that meets their needs. Like Jesus, we must be attentive to the needs around us. Needs give an entry point into the hearts and lives of others. Needs put demands upon our faith. James puts it this way.

> What good is it, my brothers, if a man claims to have faith but has no deeds?

> Can such faith save him? Suppose a
> brother or sister is without clothes
> and daily food. If one of you says to
> him, 'Go, I wish you well; keep warm
> and well fed,' but does nothing about
> his physical needs, what good is it? In
> the same way, faith by itself, if it is not
> accompanied by action, is dead.
> (James 2:14-16 NIV)

Our church name and doctrinal beliefs
mean nothing to people apart from our
taking an active interest in their needs.
The Pharisees in their day became so re-
ligiously removed from people with problems that the purpose of the church became misguided. It disturbed them that
Jesus hung-out with needy people . . .
publicans and sinners!

Matthew 9:12 "But when Jesus heard
that, he said unto them, They that be
whole need not a physician, but they that
are sick."

Jesus knew that the answer worked best
in the presence of the problem. Our light
shines brighter in the darkness.

There are churches today that are uncomfortable with their members going out
into the real world to witness. They're afraid
that the world is going to rub off on them.

To that I respond defiantly! The God that we serve is greater than the God of this world. If what the world has is able to rub off on what we have, then we better reassess whether we really have God!

In Acts 3:5, the crippled man looked to Peter and John, expecting to receive something of them. That's okay. He had a need. Perhaps he was expecting a few pennies for his next meal. How could he know that he needed Jesus? Peter and John met him there and then led him to the real answer to his problems.

The world will give you their attention when they're expecting to receive something from you. They don't know how to receive from God. You may be the closest confrontation with God that they will ever have.

One night as my partner and I walked the streets, we approached a man who was standing in the shadows of a Dairy Queen. He had watched us pray for some young people in the parking lot, so as we approached, he barked, "Don't talk to me about your God!"

We moved toward him, and he said it again. "I said, don't talk to me about your God!"

"Okay," I responded cautiously, "But what's the matter?"

"I just put my family to bed hungry tonight . . . so don't tell me that there is a God that cares," he continued.

"I've been out of work for three weeks. What kind of God would allow my children to suffer like this?"

Seeing the opportunity, I spoke confidently.

"If you can show me that you're telling the truth about your family needing food, I'll take you to the store for groceries. . . . That's the kind of God I serve."

The man was shocked. His demeanor changed.

"You would do that?" He stammered.

"Yes! Perhaps God sent us expressly to help you out. Do you live nearby?"

Anxiously, he led us a few blocks away to an old dilapidated apartment building, where his family and his brother's family were all living in the attic. Climbing up an outside fire escape, we entered the hot, dingy, attic space to discover the most deplorable conditions I had ever seen in our little town.

That night we had the joy of taking

that family to the grocery store, spend-
ing more than we planned, feeding
them, praying with them, and leading
them to the Lord Jesus Christ. There
was joy in their hearts and smiles on
their faces.

There is nothing more rewarding than
meeting someone's need and then having
them ask you, "What makes you so different!" There is joy in doing it the Jesus
way!

When you give them something that
they think they need, then you've earned
the right to give them something that you
know they need.

But too often, we carry our faith with
an edge of arrogance. We get in people's
faces with an answer that we know they
need . . . without demonstrating the love
of Christ.

We knew this family needed Jesus
Christ. They probably weren't tithing, reading their Bibles, or even going to church.
We could have discussed the reasons why
he had lost his job, but, instead, we met
him where he was . . . at the point of his
need.

Meeting needs exercises our faith. The
exercise of our faith in turn invites the

participation of the Holy Spirit. Then anything can happen! Isn't that what we want?

Putting our faith into action brings the love of Christ out of the abstract and into a reality that others can understand.

I John 3:18 "My little children, let us not love in word, neither in tongue; but in deed and truth."

Jesus said, in Matthew 25:40, "Inasmuch as ye have done it unto one of the least of these my brethren, ye have done it unto me."

Done what? Reached out to meet the tangible needs of another.

What's more, in this parable Jesus even attaches our heavenly reward with these simple acts of kindness.

> Then shall the King say unto them on his right hand, Come, ye blessed of my Father, inherit the kingdom prepared for you from the foundation of the world: For I was an hungered, and ye gave me meat: I was thirsty, and ye gave me drink: I was a stranger, and ye took me in: Naked, and ye clothed me: I was sick, and ye visited me: I was in prison, and ye came unto me. (Matt. 25:34-36)

Jesus is saying, "Do it my way . . . follow me, and I'll make you Fisher's of Men!"

Principle 2—Expect Divine Appointments

When you begin doing ministry the Jesus way, you can expect God to divinely bring you together with opportunities. I call them divine appointments . . . one-to-one meetings, divinely prearranged by God.

In John 6:44, Jesus said, "No man can come to me, except the Father which hath sent me draw him . . ."

God is at work drawing people unto Himself. We should not try to do it without Him. He is directing our steps so that we will be at the right place, at the right time, to deliver His Word into the fertile soil of a hungry heart.

It's arrogant and presumptuous for us to think that we can take our cities for Christ through clever marketing and administrative efforts. It goes against the heart of God for us to treat souls as numbers, notching our guns with short-order conversions for our own self-aggrandizement. Instead, we must pray for a deep compassion for people. We must get the heart of God and go in His authority, with a genuine love for the souls of men. We must link up with His divine plan for His church, our lives, and our cities.

Philippians 2:13 reads, "For it is God which worketh in you both to will and to do of his good pleasure."

Every time we go out on the streets to share Christ, we discover divine appointments—every time, without exception. I'm convinced that if you simply put yourself into the will of God by "going out" into the field, that God will make your efforts fruitful.

God is sending us into the world. He is sending us into the Samaria's of the world.

Samaria

In John 4:4, Jesus had to go through Samaria. He came to a town called Sychar, a name which meant "falsehood and drunkenness." Orthodox Jews of that time would deliberately walk three days out of their way to bypass Samaria.

Samaria was reproached because the people there were considered a mixed race, half-breeds. This racial prejudice made them despised by the Jews.

Jesus sat down by a well, divinely ordered by God to meet a woman there. His ministry in her life that day drew out and reached the entire town. That's God ordered evangelism! We are all called to Samaria.

"But ye shall receive power, after that the Holy Ghost is come upon you: and ye shall be witnesses unto me both in Jerusalem, and in all Judaea, and in Samaria, and unto the uttermost part of the earth" (Acts 1:8).

All Judea generally refers to an area that encompasses Samaria. Yet, in this scripture, Jesus specifically refers to Samaria, perhaps to underscore our call today.

Today our Samaria's refer to the poorly regarded or forgotten areas and the inferior or uncomfortable places. Ghettos, inner-city areas, refugee camps, rehabilitation centers, prisons, convalescent homes, hospitals . . . you must discover these in your region.

Samaria can also represent people groups, minorities, subcultures, or even those in your own families who are unlovely, hard to handle, ungrateful, or unkind.

Jesus was slandered once by being

called a Samaritan, full of the devil. Yet he often mentioned Samaria and used Samaritan people in His stories to make the point. We cannot overlook anyone. Man looks on the outward appearance, but God looks on the heart. Every man bleeds red. The world is our mission field, and every soul is precious to God.

Jesus tells a story in Luke 14 that makes it so clear.

> A certain man was preparing a great banquet and invited many guests. At the time of the banquet he sent his servant to tell those who had been invited, Come, for everything is now ready. But they all alike began to make excuses. The first said, I have just bought a field, and I must go and see it. Please excuse me. Another said, I have just bought five yoke of oxen, and I'm on my way to try them out. Please excuse me. Still another said, I just got married, so I can't come. (Luke 14:16-23 NIV)

These excuses are so typical today. The field represents real estate, property, and things that can distract us from the call of God. The five yoke of oxen could represent our love affair with automobiles today. And the last excuse, "I just got married." Satan definitely uses the struggles in marriage to distract us from the work of the Lord.

But the story continues. The servant came back and reported this to his master, who became angry and ordered his servant, "Go out quickly into the streets and alleys of the town and bring in the poor, the crippled, the blind and the lame . . . so that my house will be full."

God invites the discarded people of our generation, the drug addicts, the alcoholics, the prostitutes and people with AIDS . . . literally, society's unwanted . . . to the banqueting table. The Lord will fill his house with, "whosoever will" (Rev. 22:17).

God instructs us to go out into the Samaria's of our world, find people with needs and compel them to come in.

Principle 3—Your Mouth and God's Wisdom

"And it shall turn to you for a testimony. Settle it therefore in your hearts, not to meditate before ye shall answer: For I will give you a mouth and wisdom, which all your adversaries shall not be able to gainsay nor resist" (Luke 21:13-14).

This is a powerful promise!

Here Jesus is speaking about the last days, and He makes these profound declarations.

1. People will turn to you for a testimony. In other words, in the last days, people will be coming to you to ask what makes you so different!
2. Don't meditate on what you will say. Meaning, don't worry about having all your lines rehearsed.
3. For I will give you a mouth and wisdom—our mouth, and God's wisdom!
4. Your adversaries (enemies) won't be able to gainsay (mock you) or resist you!

Wow! I like that kind of ministry. And it's happening.

Out on the streets and in bars, I'm always amazed at how God uses me. After all, I have no background in the world. Raised in a strict Christian home, I never knew the streets or bars. I was not born with any "street smarts." Yet the Holy Spirit makes me "cool." The Holy Spirit makes me relevant.

I'm convinced that even when I say corny, "uncool" things, God can make the hearer hear what he needs to hear. Like on the day of Pentecost when the disciples were speaking in tongues, the crowd that gathered was amazed because each one heard them speaking in their own language (Acts 2:6).

Out walking the streets one night, my partner and I approached three tough-looking bikers, leaning up against the hood of a car.

"Hi guys," I said, waving my hand in a friendly salute as we approached.

"Hi guys," the fellow in the middle retorted, mocking my greeting in an effeminate tone.

I stopped directly in front of him and extended my hand up to his chest.

"Here, shake a hand," I offered.

He didn't move. His steely eyes stared into mine. Everybody froze, not knowing what might happen next. After all, it was around midnight on the roughest street in town.

I waited. It was only seconds, but it seemed longer because the air was tense. I had not planned this encounter and was determined that he make the next move.

His eyes still on me, he slowly raised his hand, spit into it, and then extended it to mine.

"Here, I have AIDS," he sneered.

I grasped his hand. Glancing at it, I noticed it was covered with ugly scabs. I don't think he had AIDS. I think he was just trying to shake me.

"What are you guys doing out on this street at night?" he asked.

"Just walking," I replied. "What are you doing?"

"We live here," he scowled, then continued.

"You know you can get anything you want out here." Gesturing towards a passing prostitute, he commented further.

"You want her? You can have her!"

I changed the subject, asked him what he did for a living, and soon we were conversing on common ground. But most importantly, I stayed. Twenty minutes later we were chatting like friends. My opening line was "uncool," but the Spirit of God could not be denied. A few weeks later we got to pray with two of those men, and one came to know Christ as savior. Praise the Lord!

The encounter illustrates my point.

Stop worrying about how to do it. Stop worrying about what you will say. In the proverbial words of Nike, "Just do it!"

Allow God to have the opportunity to do it through you.

I never felt fear during that experience. When you're doing the work of God, you receive His strength and safety. In fact, the safest place in the world to be is in the will of God!

Principle 4—Demonstrate the Power

There comes a time in every ministry opportunity when you have to stop talking and start doing!

People today are looking for us to put-up or shut-up!

The Apostle Paul himself said, in I Corinthians 2:4, "My speech and my preaching were not with enticing words of man's wisdom, but in demonstration of the Spirit and of power."

Demonstration is what people are looking for.

The church has done well in the area of information. We've also done well in the area of inspiration. But today is a day for demonstration!

Step out and put what you know to the test. Lay your hands on somebody, and see what the Lord will do.

"Well, what if nothing happens?" you might ask.

Well, so what. What if it does happen?

If you do nothing, you'll never be wrong, but you'll never be right either. Step out. Do something!

When my mind tries to tell me, "What if it doesn't work?" God reminds me not to worry about quality control.

I hear Him say, "You're in sales. You just show the plan. You just speak the words. Let me worry about whether the product will perform to the manufacturer's specifications. My Word says it will! Let me take care of that!"

You can talk until you're blue in the face, but to reach today's lost generation, the Spirit has to move. Actually the gifts of the Spirit work better in the secular world than in the sanctuary because that's who they were given for.

Jesus demonstrated the Spirit's power to the Samaritan woman in John 4:19 through a word of revelation. His supernatural knowledge of her past five husbands awakened her to spiritual reality.

"*Sir,*" the woman said, "I perceive that you are a prophet."

In every witnessing opportunity, we should watch for the right moment to demonstrate the Spirit's power through a word of revelation, the laying on of hands, or prayer for the sick.

I have found that the supernatural operates in greater power and more precision on the streets, in the bars, or wherever else the darkness of sin rules. This will only happen when we are willing to stop talking and start acting in faith.

One night on a downtown street, I noticed a young man sitting alone on some steps. I sat beside him, ignoring his cold, hostile response.

I talked. He listened, in silence, until I said something that caught his attention.

"Did you say God spoke to you?" he asked. He insisted on an explanation, and as I responded, tears flowed down his face. "I wish God would speak to me," he said wistfully.

I prayed that he would hear God's voice in the coming days. Not long after, God did speak to him in a series of dreams, and today the man serves faithfully in the church.

Enough of our clinical, doctrinal approaches to Christianity. Our mission, should we choose to accept it, is to minister the Jesus way—like He did with the woman at the well. Take time with people. Show genuine concern. Offer prayer. Prayer invites touch and the opportunity for divine impartation . . . then anything can happen.

God desires it. Your faith triggers it. Now expect it!

4.

UNDERSTANDING OUR MISSION

We are on a mission, should we choose to accept it. And it's not Mission Impossible. God intends for us to fulfill it before Christ returns.

According to Matthew 24:14, "And this gospel of the kingdom shall be preached in all the world for a witness unto all nations; and then shall the end come."

As a church and Christian nation, we have lost sight of our mission. The word *mission* immediately conjures up thoughts of overseas ministry exploits, but I'm not talking about going anywhere. I'm talking about the assignment given to us by God.

The last words of Jesus before He ascended to heaven are seen in Mark 16:15, "And he said unto them, Go ye into all the world, and preach the gospel to every creature."

This passage, often referred to as the Great Commission, has largely become the Great Omission. We know what it says and what it means, but we simply are not doing it.

"Go ye" simply means, you go! These words are spoken to all of us as disciples of Jesus Christ. This is spoken as a command, not just to evangelists, but to every obedient follower of Jesus Christ. Never has a command been so analyzed, rationalized, mystified, or compromised. A hyperbole-parable takeoff on Matthew 4:19 says it well.

Modern Day Parable on Evangelism

Now it came to pass that a group existed who called themselves fishermen. And, lo, there were many fish in waters all around. Streams and lakes were filled with fish, and they were all very hungry.

Week after week, month after month, year after year, people who called themselves fishermen met in meetings and talked about their call to fish. They talked about the abundance of fish and how they really should go fishing. They built large buildings for local fishing headquarters and issued pleas on a regular basis for more fishermen. But they didn't fish.

They organized a Board to send out fishermen to other places where there were many fish. Their great vision and courage to speak out about fishing was seen in their promotion brochures and spirited rallies to wish these fishermen well. But the staff and committee members just never got around to fishing.

Large, elaborate training centers were built to teach fishermen how to fish. Persons with doctorates in "fishology" were hired to do the teaching. But all they did was teach fishing . . . they didn't fish.

After one stirring meeting on "The Necessity of Fishing," one young fellow left the meeting and went fishing. He caught two outstanding fish. He was honored for his excellent catch and was immediately scheduled to visit all the big meetings to tell about his experience. So, he quit fishing to travel about, telling his story.

Now, there were people around them who questioned their status as fishermen and laughed at their clubs and rallies, since there was never any evidence of any fish being brought in. But they continued claiming to be fishermen, even if they never found time to fish.

Jesus said, "Follow me, and I will make you fishers of men" (Matt. 4:19).

The World and the Church

Jesus commands us to go into the world. "For God so loved the world, that He gave . . ." Jesus gave His life for the world, not for the church. The devil has tricked us into leaving the world alone because it is in darkness.

As children of Light, God has equipped us to penetrate darkness . . . but we have to GO there. Jesus said, "Ye are the Light of the world . . ." (Matt. 5:14).

We hear the cliché, "The lights are on but nobody's home." For the church it would be, "Somebody's home but the lights aren't on."

We've become too busy with church to be concerned with the world. We've gotten sidetracked. The church is not supposed to be our mission. Jesus never asked us to build the church. He said, "I will build my Church . . ." (Matt. 16:18).

Actually, WE ARE the church, and we can't build ourselves.

Our mission then is to touch the world. To do that we must simply *be* the church. We must be the church in the world. We must not become more occupied with the church than with the world.

The World Is Waiting

We are living in a time of deep spiritual hunger. The world is desperately looking for answers. There is a sense of spiritual need, evidenced by the enormous rise of psychics on television.

"For the earnest expectation of the creature waiteth for the manifestation of the sons of God" (Rom. 8:19).

This tells us that all of creation is waiting in earnest expectation for the emergence of a people who truly look like, talk like, and act like sons of God. The world is looking for an answer to come from God's people. We are those people!

Verses 20-21 tell us that God, Himself, has subjected the world to vanity (disappointing misery and frustration) in the hope that they would be drawn to the glorious liberty of the children of God and be delivered from their bondage. The world is waiting for us. God is waiting for us. There is an earnest expectation that what we have is truly genuine. Perhaps it's time for us to step up to the plate, grow up, and arise to the call that is obviously upon us.

So what is the world waiting for? We're here. There's a church on practically every street corner. Why don't they come in and discover the truth?

Ghandi once said, "If the world could meet the Christ of Christianity, they would believe in Him. But, they have met the Christians of Christ, and have rejected Him."

The world is not attracted to the Light of Christ in us because we are not shining. We are not being the church. We are more like children than we are good sons and daughters. There is a difference.

Romans 8:14 says, "For as many as are led by the Spirit of God, they are the sons of God."

Romans 8:16 reads, "The Spirit itself beareth witness with our spirit, that we are the children of God."

A comparison of the Greek words used here in these two verses to understand sons of God and children of God gives us our answer.

The Greek word for "children" in verse 16 is *teknon*, which literally refers to a relationship established by birth.

The Greek word for "sons" in verse 14 is *huios,* which is a term more often used to denote function or activity of the child within the family. Those who are "led by the Spirit," are doing something and going somewhere. They are hearing and obeying the commands of the Father. They are true sons.

In other words, we are children by birth, or rather, by rebirth, but we become good sons through obedience to our Father's business.

Understanding what Father's business is should be our utmost desire. We want to become good sons and daughters. It's what God desires of us, and it's what the world is waiting for... with earnest expectation.

Simply believing in God is not enough. The Bible says that even the devils believe ... so much that they tremble (James 2:19). But they do not act on their belief. That is where faith comes in.

II Timothy 3:5 speaks of a last days form of godliness that denies the power of God by "ever learning, and never able to come to the knowledge of the truth." How can you be "ever learning," but never coming to the knowledge you need?

Again, there are two different Greek

words used for the word *knowledge*. One
speaks of an academic understanding while
here the Greek word is *epignosis,* speaking
of a participative or experiential knowledge.

In other words, these are people who
are ever learning, academically, but never
applying that knowledge in a participative way. They are ever learning but never
doing anything with it! You are the evidence of God's reality on the earth today.
What are you doing to supply that evidence? Simply believing in Him is not
enough. It takes faith to step out and do
something. Hebrews 11:6 tells us that without faith it is impossible to please God.
He wants us to step out in faith. And, He
gives us the authority to step out.

The Great Commission calls us to a
mission with the granted authority and
power to fulfill that mission. Look at the
word by definition:

> COM = The granted authority and
> power to do.
> MISSION = A particular task or duty.

"But ye are a chosen generation, a royal
priesthood, an holy nation, a peculiar
people; that ye should shew forth the

praises of him who hath called you out of darkness into his marvelous light" (I Pet. 2:9).

"But God hath chosen the foolish things of the world to confound the wise; and God hath chosen the weak things of the world to confound the things which are mighty" (I Cor. 1:27).

"Ye have not chosen me, but I have chosen you, and ordained you, that ye should go and bring forth fruit, and that your fruit should remain: that whatsoever ye shall ask of the Father in my name, he may give it you" (John 15:16).

"Who also hath made us able ministers of the new testament; not of the letter, but of the spirit: for the letter killeth, but the spirit giveth life" (II Cor. 3:6).

A Test of Faith

We have been called, commisioned, and equipped to fulfill the Great Commission. It's time that we step out in faith and begin thinking, talking, and acting like true sons and daughters of God!

Jesus said in Mark 9:23, "If thou canst believe, all things are possible to him that believeth."

Perhaps the real question is, do we really believe? Does our faith show that we believe?

I'm challenged by the example of the Canaanite woman coming to Jesus in Matthew 15:22. "Have mercy on me, O Lord, thou son of David: my daughter is grievously vexed with a devil," she cried.

At first, Jesus didn't even answer her. In fact, his disciples implored Him to send her away because she had been persistently pursuing them.

Then Jesus responded with a rather negative word, explaining that His ministry was first to the Jew and that it was premature for Him to be performing miracles for Gentiles. He even referred to her as a "dog," a familiar but demeaning reference to Gentiles in those days.

"It is not meet to take the children's bread, and cast it to dogs," He said. Meaning, it's not right for me to give what rightfully belongs to the children of Israel to those who are not under the covenant blessing of God.

"Truth, Lord," she replied. "Yet the dogs eat of the crumbs which fall from their master's table." Verse 25 says that she worshipped Him. The word here in the Greek is *proskuneo,* meaning that she threw herself prostrate at His feet, like a dog giving adoring homage to its master.

This woman got serious with God!

Verse 28 records the dramatic conclusion. "Then Jesus answered and said unto her, O woman, great is thy faith: be it unto thee even as thou wilt. And her daughter was made whole from that very hour."

This Canaanite woman squeezed her miracle from the crumbs. It's like she was saying, "I'll wait for the crumbs Lord, but I won't go away!" She wouldn't take no for an answer, and she got her request granted.

We have more than crumbs available to us! We have our own place setting at the table, and yet we don't act like we truly believe.

Oh, Ye of Little Faith

One evening in our home, as we were preparing for supper, my daughter, Michelle, came to me complaining of a stomach ache. She didn't feel like eating. I directed her to her bedroom to lie down, and I proceeded to pray over her. After all, I was the man of God in the house and had a job to do.

I prayed fervently, binding and loosing, in the name of Jesus, through His shed blood, quoting I Peter 2:24, "By whose stripes ye were healed." I laid hands on her head, her feet, and hands, taking authority over the spirit of infirmity and making declaration of God's healing touch.

Then I left the room, feeling pretty pleased with myself.

A few minutes later, little Michelle came traipsing back out to the kitchen. This time with a smile on her face. "Michelle, were you just fooling daddy?" I asked, surprised that she was back already.

"No daddy, I'm healed!" she said gleefully.

At that immediate moment, I distinctly heard the Spirit of God say to me, "Oh ye of little faith! You went through all the motions but didn't really believe that it would happen!"

Ouch! That was a strong word. Especially for a preacher.

Good God!

I remember the story of a young boy riding his broken skateboard out in front of the preacher's house. The wheels kept coming off, and each time, in his frustration, the little boy would say "Good God!"

The preacher watched for a while until

he couldn't take it any more. Then he approached the boy.

"Son," he said, "You shouldn't be using that kind of language. When the wheels fly off, just say Praise the Lord!"

"Well, okay," was the boy's reply, rather matter-a-fact.

He skated a little further, and the wheels flew off again. "Praise the Lord," the boy exclaimed. Immediately the wheels miraculously returned to their axles.

"Good God!" the preacher blurted!

Sometimes even preachers go through all the motions without truly believing that God will perform the miracle!

Hollywood

Secular Hollywood movies speak out, giving us a pulse on what the world is looking for.

Some years ago, when the movie, *Leap of Faith,* came out, I was told that lead actor Steve Martin understudied Benny Hinn to learn his character. The story was about a phony faith healer who traveled about holding tent revivals in small towns, preying on vulnerable people. Jannette and I went to see the movie, expecting the worst. After all, Steve Martin is a comedian, and this was a Hollywood movie.

Some parts were hard to endure, but we were surprised to see how the story progressed and what the movie was actually saying. While Martin's character applied his deceptive trickery before the crowds, God moved in and performed a genuine miracle. This so bewildered and awed the phony tent preacher that he quit and left town. The final scenes showed the tent revival going on strong, through the faith of true believers and without a preacher.

Hollywood was saying, "We know that there is counterfeit, and yet we believe there is a genuine. If the genuine is out there will it please stand up!"

There was the popular movie sequel, *Sister Act*, starring Whoopie Goldberg. Goldberg played the role of a nightclub singer who was temporarily placed in a nun's convent under a witness protection program.

While there, she questioned the relevance of the church to the real world and encouraged the nuns to get out into the streets and discover the needs of people. She also fired up the church choir with a contemporary, energetic, music style that caused church attendance to swell to standing room only, culminating in a personal visit from the Pope himself.

These movies are crying out for the church to be relevant and compassionate toward the society in which we live.

The world's answers have fallen short. There is no pill for AIDS. There is no lasting cure for drug addiction or alcoholism. Depression is at an epidemic high. More and more the world is recognizing the need for a spiritual solution. There is a vacuum of spiritual need in every man that only Jesus can fill.

The Groaning

The world is groaning with hunger for change. This groaning of hunger for change is creating an atmosphere in which God can move.

Romans 8:22-23 says,

> For we know that the whole creation groaneth and travaileth in pain together until now. And not only they, but ourselves also, which have the firstfruits of the Spirit, even we ourselves groan with ourselves, waiting for the adoption, to wit, the redemption of our body.

The groaning sound is a time indicator. God is about to do something.

Remember in Exodus 2:24, when God heard the groaning of the children of Israel, He remembered His covenant with Abraham and went into action. Immediately we read of God manifesting himself to Moses through the burning bush. This marked the end of forty years that Moses spent in the desert of preparation.

David speaks prophetically when he writes in Psalms 102:19-20, "For he hath looked down from the height of his sanctuary; from heaven did the Lord behold the earth; To hear the groaning of the prisoner; to loose those that are appointed to death."

The world is groaning in pain and travail, searching for an answer. If the church doesn't step forward with an answer, others will. Hopeless, misguided people are only too willing to follow celebrity psychics on TV, self-gratifying cult leaders like David Koresh, or even images of the Virgin Mary on a wall.

Virgin Mary

In 1996, hundreds of thousands of people flocked to Clearwater, Florida, just a few miles from our Christian Retreat Center in Bradenton, to view an image that resembled the Virgin Mary, glowing from the glass wall of a high-rise office building. People came hoping for healings or inner spiritual comfort.

> A local newspaper editor aptly wrote, Whether the image is indeed a miraculous apparition or a natural phenomenon such as water stains from the sprinkler system, this story is a striking illustration of how hungry people are for a spiritual connection—for something to believe in that transcends this materialistic, violent world.

The church today does not have a bad reputation. Our problem is simply that we have no reputation. We do our thing every Sunday, and the world does theirs. We go through the motions of religious practice hidden inside the four walls of our comfortable church houses while the world looks for spirituality in all the wrong places. The church is largely being ignored or unnoticed by society. It's time for the Church to stand up, step out, and get noticed for God.

5.

THE CHURCH AS A FORCE

Our nation was originally founded upon Biblical principles with the church as a strong driving force. Today, however, the church has little influence upon modern society.

Our school system reaches out for more and more authority in the lives of our children, ignoring the church and family as the primary source of teaching values. Respect for clergy as religious professionals deteriorates amidst repeated national scandals of televangelists.

God never intended it to be this way. God intended for the church to be a powerful force to be reckoned with. In the words of Jesus, "I will build my church; and the gates of Hell shall not prevail against it" (Matt. 16:18).

At the heart of this collapse is a slow deterioration of the heart of the church itself. Living, vibrant passion has given way to passive, complacent institution. Without the fire of human passion, the church becomes merely an edifice of bricks and mortar.

What began in the Spirit has become flesh. What began high in vision and poorly funded has become a well-funded, but dying institution.

"Are ye so foolish? Having begun in the Spirit, are ye now made perfect by the flesh?" (Gal. 3:3)

But wait. There's a Light on the horizon. There are pockets of resistance fighting the status quo and raising up a strong and vibrant army of God in these last days.

God is once again raising up men of Issachar (I Chron. 12:32), who have an understanding of the times and are not bound by tradition and the past, people who know what the church ought to do, people who are hearing God and acting upon His Word. He is raising up a people who know what the ministry of the church is and understand that it is extended through every member of the body (Eph. 4:16) "the whole body fitly joined together." They understand that ministry is assisted and released by the pastor "equipping the saints for ministry" (Eph. 4:12).

There are three forceful ministries in the church today.

1. Ministry to the Lord (Worship)
2. Ministry to the body (Fellowship)
3. Ministry to the world (Evangelism)

These three ministries are ordered . . .

> in priority
> in plurality
> in trinity

facilitated by . . .

> God the Father
> Jesus His Son
> the Holy Spirit

Ministry to the Lord

Ministry to the Lord is our opportunity to worship our Creator. It is an opportunity for developing relationship with God. What an awesome privilege to actually minister to God. This ministry to the Lord should not be seen merely as an activity, but as the key to releasing the power of the Holy Spirit.

"As they ministered to the Lord, and fasted the Holy Ghost said. . . " (Acts 13:2).

God speaks when we are attentive to Him.

There are two things that our ministry to the Lord does:

1) Establishes relationship. As we worship we find that we decrease and He increases. Actually, your desire to worship the Lord is proof positive of your conversion. Mechanical prayer unto salvation alone does not save. The real question is are you worshipping the Lord.

2) Creates power for miracles. In Matthew 15:25, the Gentile woman with the demonized daughter did not get a response from Jesus until she worshipped Him. Our worship moves the heart of God, even to the point of changing His timetable.

Ministry to the Body

Our ministry to one another is very special in God's sight. Our fellowship with one another should not be taken lightly. I'm not speaking of shallow, superficial handshaking and backslapping.

The word in the Greek is *koinonia,* meaning "to share in common." Acts 2:44-45 says, "And all that believed were together, and had all things common; and sold their possessions and goods, and parted them to all men, as every man had need."

I John 1:7 simply says, "If we walk in the light, as He is in the light, we have fellowship one with another. . . ."

God's Word even calls fellowship a sacrifice like unto the sacrifice of praise. Immediately following the familiar verse Hebrews 13:15, which speaks of the "sacrifice of praise to God . . . that is the fruit of our lips, giving thanks to His name," we read about another sacrifice. It's the sacrifice of koinonia.

Hebrews 13:16, "But to do good and to communicate *(koinonia)* forget not; for with such sacrifices God is well pleased."

These two scriptures speak of the sacrifices of praise and koinonia. True fellowship is open, honest, transparent, and trusting and, I might add, it's rather rare in the body of Christ today.

Ministry to the World

A natural by-product of a healthy church, nourished through worship and fellowship, is the ministry of evangelism. Soul winning and evangelism results from a healthy relationship with the Lord, because it comes out of personal revelation.

I John 1:1-3, expresses the excitement of the disciples who shared from firsthand experience, ". . . which we have heard, which we have seen with our own eyes, which we have looked upon and our hands have handled . . . and was manifested unto us; That which we have seen and heard declare we unto you."

Let us dedicate ourselves to the task of awakening the body of Christ to this Holy Spirit led ministry of evangelism.

Time of Shaking

We are living in a time and season of great shaking for the church. It's an opportunity for change. The change of ideas, attitudes, habit patterns, plans, and purposes. The shaking is intended to make us less self-centered and more God-centered.

Hebrews 12:26-27 (NIV), "Once more I will shake not only the earth, but also the heavens." The words once more indicate the removing of what can be shaken—that is, created things—so that what cannot be shaken may remain.

According to Romans 1:18 (NIV), "The wrath of God is being revealed from heaven against all the ungodliness and wickedness of men who suppress the truth by their wickedness." God is purging the church. A spiritual house is being built, as the flesh house (self) is broken.

> But we have this treasure in jars of clay to show that this all-surpassing power is from God and not from us. We are hard pressed on every side, but not crushed; perplexed, but not in despair; Persecuted, but not abandoned; struck down, but not destroyed. We always carry around in our body the death of Jesus, so that the life of Jesus may also be revealed in our body. (II Cor. 4:7-10 NIV)

> Then verse 16-18 (NIV) sums it up. Therefore we do not lose heart. Though outwardly we are wasting away, yet inwardly we are being renewed day by day. For our light and momentary troubles are achieving for us an eternal glory that far outweighs them all. So we fix our eyes not on what is seen, but on what is unseen. For what is seen is temporary, but what is unseen is eternal.

This time and season upon the church is intended to turn the hearts of God's people toward God's plan and purpose. His purpose is a militant one. There is a spiritual war going on, and God wants His army ready. This is not the season of wedding gowns, but rather for military fatigues.

The shaking in the Last Days is intended to keep us fresh and on guard. It's intended to keep us from getting stagnant.

Jeremiah 48:10-12 (NIV) gives us a picture of this God-sent shaking.

> A curse on him who is lax in doing the LORD'S work! A curse on him who keeps his sword from bloodshed! Moab has been at rest from youth, like wine left on its dregs, not poured from one jar to another—she has not gone into exile. So she tastes as she did, and her aroma is unchanged. "But days are coming," declares the LORD, "when I will send men who pour from jars, and they will pour her out; they will empty her jars and smash her jugs."

Moab is a picture of the church, at ease and complacent like wine left on its dregs. If there is not a pouring from jar to jar, the taste remains unchanged and the aroma or scent becomes rotten. God promises to send the shaking. King James Version references these movers and shakers as "wanderers" or tilters, perhaps referencing people that God sends into your life to shake you and stir you.

The trumpet has sounded, the battle is raging and yet many churches are sitting at ease. Jeremiah characterizes this superficial, lazy group of play actors in Jeremiah 5:21 and to the end of the chapter.

He speaks of this foolish and senseless people as those with eyes but do not see, who have ears but do not hear. A people with stubborn and rebellious hearts. Wicked men whose houses are full of deceit. They've become rich and powerful and have grown fat and sleek, but "they do not plead the case of the fatherless to win it, they do not defend the rights of the poor."

Verses 30-31 make these glaring observations. "A horrible and shocking thing has happened in the land: The prophets prophesy lies, the priest's rule by their own authority, and my people love it this way. But what will you do in the end?"

These strong words by Jeremiah are an indictment on the church today.

But the shocking revelation that Jeremiah brings out is that the people seem to love it this way. There is so little fear of God. There is so much compromise.

Joel blows the trumpet and sounds the alarm, calling the church to repentance, to an urgency in the Last Days, and not business as usual.

Joel 2:12 (NIV) says, "Even now," declares the Lord, "return to me with all your heart, with fasting and weeping and mourning. Rend your heart and not your garments. Return to the Lord your God. . . . "

God is shaking and God is testing.

James 1:12 (NIV) says, "Blessed is the man who perseveres under trial, because when he has stood the test, he will receive the crown of life that God has promised to those who love him."

Gideon's Test

We can better understand God's testing and selection process through a review of Gideon's army, Judges 6 and 7.

God began by calling Gideon, a rather unlikely, ordinary man. When Gideon called together his army of thirty-two thousand men, God said it was too many. Perhaps, he saw too much flesh or too much self-centeredness.

In Judges 7:3, God instructed Gideon to send home anyone who was fearful. I'm

sure that made sense to Gideon, because
he didn't want any scaredy cats in his army
anyway. He couldn't have been prepared,
however, for the mass exodus that followed.
Twenty-two thousand men were fearful and
went home.

In Judges 7:4 we read, "But the Lord
said to Gideon, There are still too many
men. Take them down to the water, and I
will sift them for you there."

God said, have them drink and pass
before me and I will sort them out. Ninety-
seven hundred of them failed the test by
laying down their weapons so they would
feel more comfortable while drinking. Only
three hundred scooped the water with one
hand and held their weapons with the
other, remaining vigilant and on guard.

The spiritual application goes like this.
Christians today have gotten lazy. God's
people are sprawled out on the riverbank,
selfishly drinking at the river of life each
time the church doors are open. Their
Bibles and spiritual weapons are out of
reach, and they are vulnerable to enemy
attack without a clue to the war that is
around them.

Let's look at weapons of warfare. In
Judges 7:16 (NIV), Gideon placed "trum-

pets and empty jars in the hands of all of them, with torches inside."

These are quite unconventional tools of battle. Each soldier has a trumpet, sho-far in one hand and a clay pot with a smoldering torch inside in the other.

Gideon's instructions on the battle plan were sketchy. "Follow my lead . . . do exactly as I do." And then he instructed them on when to blow the trumpet and shout. Interestingly, he never gave them instructions about smashing the pot.

I can hear somebody saying, "Hey, Gideon, what about the jars?"

But Gideon simply said, "Do exactly as I do." Nobody likes to have their pot broken.

Herein lies the spiritual principle. The clay pot must be broken to let the light shine out. That clay pot represents your flesh, your will, bad attitudes, anger, unforgiveness, and sin. The light of Christ simply won't shine until the clay pot is broken.

"But we have this treasure in jars of clay to show that this all surpassing power is from God and not from us" (II Cor. 4:7 NIV).

The clay pot is not a weapon of war.

It's what's inside that counts. You may think you look right or talk right or smell right, but remember, it is what is inside that counts.

Finally, God's battle plan required that the army position themselves on the edge of the enemy camp and in the middle of the night. We have to get into enemy territory. Here is where the light of Christ will bring true victory.

The final result of Gideon's spirit-led battle strategy was that the enemy turned on themselves.

Jesus said, "Occupy, till I come" (Luke 19:13). "Occupy" is a military term. It means to go into enemy territory and seize and hold until backup reinforcements come. God is birthing a church of strength and power, with a plan of winning a great victory in these Last Days. We are in a time of transition. The baby is being birthed, and we feel the pain.

Transition

Transition is a medical term, which speaks of the period of time when the baby is in the birth canal and the mother is just about to give birth. My wife, Jannette, and I learned this term when we were taking natural childbirth classes together before the birth of our first child. We were told that transition would be the most intense time of the birthing process. This would be the time of the most intense pain for the mother and with the pain, there would be disorientation and despair.

Even with the advanced training, I was not prepared for the intensity of those moments. Trying to be a good father and coach, I stood by my wife through the labor reading the monitors and instructing her in her breathing.

Those moments were precious, but when transition came, her demeanor changed. "Get out of my face, I don't want to do this any more. I quit, let's stop, I'm tired," were some of her words. But guess what? That baby was coming, like it or not. The birthing process was in its final stages, and that baby wanted out!

God's birthing process is upon the Church today. "I will build my church, and the gates of hell will not prevail against it." We're in the final stages of preparation. The devil has unleashed the hordes of hell against the Church. God's process of shaking and testing is upon us. We've felt the pain, the fatigue, and even despair. Battle weary as she may be, the Church is coming forth, knowing her God, and doing great exploits (Dan. 4:32).

God has a plan for the Church, and the devil will not prevail against it!

You are living in a time and season of God's plan for your life. Ecclesiastes 8:5 says, "A wise man's heart discerneth both time and judgment." Daniel 2:21 says, "He [God] changes the times and the seasons."

Jesus scolded the Pharisees in Luke 12:56, "Ye hypocrites, ye can discern the face of the sky and of the earth; but how is it that ye do not discern this time?"

In Luke 19:41-44, we see that Jesus looked over the city of Jerusalem and wept over it, ". . . because thou knewest not the time of thy visitation."

When people don't move in the timing and seasons of God they are vulnerable to the enemies temptation. Be careful not to become too comfortable. This is not a maintenance ministry. God intends for us to plow the ground and move with the cloud and the seasons.

In II Samuel 11:1, King David missed the timing and season of battle. "And it came to pass, after the year was expired, at the time when kings go forth to battle . . . David tarried still at Jerusalem."

The verses that follow walk us down a path of temptation, adultery, concealment of sin, and ultimately murder. All of which weaved its way into David's life because he was sitting at home when it was time to be on the battlefront.

God is shaking and testing. He's building His remnant army. A spiritual house is being built as our house of flesh and self is broken. Outwardly, we are wasting away so that inwardly we can be renewed.

A dear friend of mine, Albert, is in prison paying a harsh penalty for a drug-related crime. He calls me once or twice every week, and God is doing such wonderful things in his spiritual life. He works closely with the chaplain of the prison and ministers to other men at every opportunity. Each time he calls me, he speaks about the Lord and amplifies the scriptures with revelation knowledge, always joyful, always growing. Just three years into a fifty-seven year sentence, he recently made this statement. "No time I've spent here has been wasted. I'm growing spiritually and putting down deep roots. My whole perspective has been changed."

My eyes watered as he spoke, and I

remembered the scripture in Hebrews 12:11 (NIV), "No discipline seems pleasant at the time, but painful. Later on, however, it produces a harvest of righteousness and peace for those who have been trained by it."

Hear the word of the Lord. There is a call to build the house of the Lord. It's a spiritual house built with the living stones of man (I Pet. 2:4-5).

Haggai

The prophet, Haggai, sounded the alarm to the people of his generation. A people, who through disobedience had become lethargic, self-centered, indifferent and complacent. The foundation of the temple had been laid, but the work was halted for fear of their enemies. The project was aborted.

The words of the prophet hit close to home as he writes,

> Is it a time for you yourself to be living in your paneled houses, while this house remains a ruin? Now this is what the Lord Almighty says: Give careful thought to your ways. You have planted much, but have har-

vested little. You eat, but never have
enough. You drink, but never have
your fill. You put on clothes, but are
not warm. You earn wages only to
put them in a purse with holes in it.
This is what the Lord Almighty says:
Give careful thought to your ways.
(Hag. 1:4-7 NIV)

Haggai gave seven Last Days commands from the Lord Almighty.

1) Consider your ways, give careful
   thought. Four times this was said.
2) Go up to the mountain (prayer)
   for building supplies.
3) Build the house (our spiritual
   house).
4) Be strong.
5) Fear not.
6) Ask the priest what the law says
   and hunger for holiness.
7) Give careful thought from this day
   on; look expectantly to the future.

The Scriptures say in verse twelve that
the whole remnant of the people obeyed
the voice of the Lord when they heard
Haggai's message. The blessing of God
came when they obeyed and began to
work.

A Vessel of Honor

II Timothy 2:20-21, speaks of vessels
of honor and vessels of dishonor. "But in
a great house there are not only vessels of
gold and of silver, but also of wood and of
earth; and some to honor, and some to
dishonor. If a man therefore purge himself from these, he shall be a vessel unto
honor, sanctified, and meet for the master's
use, and prepared unto every good work."

The revelation of this scripture goes
beyond the obvious. Obviously vessels of
gold and silver are considered of greater
value than those of wood and of earth.

However, the context here is that one
is made noble by USE and not by appearance. One is made noble by being
cleansed, holy, and prepared, "meat for
the master's use and prepared unto every
good work."

In my own house we have two sets of
dishes. One set is within easy reach and
used every day, made of a cheaper but
more durable plastic material. The other
set is in the china cabinet, rarely used,
finely crafted of bone china, etched in gold.
This set we wouldn't dare use regularly for
fear of breaking it.

Many pew-sitting Christians live their

lives this way, beautifully on display each week in the sanctuary, but of little useful value out on the mission field of everyday life. They are more concerned about their appearance than their usefulness.

God is not really interested in polishing and making bigger and better earthen vessels. He wants us to be prepared unto every good work. Besides it's the treasure inside the vessel that really counts. And when a vessel begins to look too good, it refuses to be broken. Remember, it's only when the old clay pot is broken, that the light of Christ can really shine out.

A missionary friend, Russell Stendahl, was a casual Christian, a preacher's kid who was too busy for God. Until one day, he was kidnapped by Columbian drug lords. For 142 days he sat tied to a tree in a jungle with a rope around his neck. It was his wake-up call. God got his attention and made his heart soft for the ministry.

Eric Highsmith was a young athlete, with a promising future, but running from God. One day in a tragic car accident, he lost his left leg. Today, Eric shares candidly how the accident drew him back to the Lord. As a testimony of God's grace,

Eric plays professional tennis on one leg, assisted by a specially designed crutch and tennis racket. He also travels extensively sharing his testimony and encouraging other young people not to be self-centered, but to recognize that God has a call upon their lives.

The Last Days Church

The church of the Last Days will have four distinguishing characteristics.

1) A Praying Church

II Chronicles 7:14 says, "If my people, which are called by my name, shall humble themselves, and pray, and seek my face, and turn from their wicked ways; then will I hear from heaven, and will forgive their sin, and will heal their land."

There is nothing like adversity to cause people to call upon God. The New Testament church was born in adversity.

I'll never forget a particular airplane trip where the air turbulence was so bad that we weren't sure if we were going to make it. At thirty thousand feet up in the sky, people felt helpless, and their thoughts went heavenward.

Many screamed out to God without

embarrassment or inhibition. Like somebody once said, "There are no atheists in a crashing airplane!"

The adversities of the Last Days are drawing us closer to God. That difficulty you're having is an opportunity for a closer relationship with God. Talk to Him about it.

I know that as a father, the best opportunity I have to build a relationship with my children is when they skin their knees and come to me for comfort. When my daughter, Michelle, was learning to ride a two wheel bicycle for the first time, her independent spirit didn't want any help from daddy. She straddled the bike and walked it down the driveway by herself.

Watching from a window inside the house, I saw her take a tumble at the end of the drive. Leaving the bicycle behind, she walked all the way back to the house to climb up into Daddy's lap for comfort and reassurance.

This is the kind of relationship that God longs to have with His children. The adversity in these Last Days is drawing us into the arms of God and also drawing us closer to one another. It's no longer a select group of people coming together for church services to promote doctrine and theology. But at a grass-roots level, we're becoming a living, active, caring group of people who reach out to one another's needs.

2) A Spiritual Church

Once our flesh has been tested, tried and purged, we lose some weight and become more spiritually healthy. John the Baptist said, "He must increase, but I must decrease" (John 3:30).

Gideon heard the Word of the Lord and did four things to prepare his remnant army:

1. Worshipped God. This is the place to start in all our battles.
2. He spoke the word. "Get up for the Lord has given you the city."
3. He divided them up and organized them. Spiritually this represents the complete use of the fivefold ministry and freedom of the gifts of the spirit.
4. He placed unconventional tools of battle in their hands.

God wants us to get off our "blessed assurance" and move on to embrace and fulfill His purpose for our being here on the earth. Jesus came to earth on a mission. He fulfilled His mission and then announced ours. We must embrace this mission with an expectation of fulfilling it to usher in the return of Christ.

3) A Warring Church

The church in the Last Days will become more confrontational, no longer just letting things happen, but standing up to be a voice for biblical standards and godly morality.

Social issues like legalized abortions, pornography, homosexuality, sexual promiscuity, drug addictions, and alcoholism are all issues that the church must take a stand on. Without strong conviction, compromise will set in.

While the Presbyterian church drops the hymn "Onward Christian Soldiers" because of its militancy, and the Episcopal church agrees to ordaining homosexual ministers, there is a church arising with fire in its wings. Churches like David Wilkerson's Times Square Church, a seventeen hundred seat opera house style theater, carved out of the center of the inner-city where people assemble despite the concern about getting their car stolen, dismantled, or even themselves mugged.

Another example of great inner-city churches is Tommy Barnett's Los Angeles International Church which crosses ethnic and nationality barriers by offering a worship experience in eight or ten different languages.

There is something else that I learned in natural childbirth classes. The instructors taught a method for dealing with the pain of the transition period. It's called focal point.

They encouraged us to bring a family photograph into the delivery room and strategically place it in easy eyesight of the mother. When the pain of childbirth got so intense that the mother began losing focus and concentration, she was encouraged to make the family photograph her focal point.

Instead of thrashing about wildly, without focus, she was to remind herself of the reason why she was doing what she was doing. Her family and the joyful expectation of her newborn child would help her endure the pain.

Soul winning is the focal point for the church today. The church that turns its attention towards soul winning has locked in on God's highest priority. It brings focus and purpose to the church, and it actually helps to relieve the pain of these troubled times. The Bible is full of promises and rewards for those who turn their attention toward the needs of others.

In a nation where most Americans think there is no such thing as absolute truth and believe that people of different religions all worship the same God, the church desperately needs a focal point.

George Barner of the Barner Research Group in Glendale, California, conducted a survey that shows that traditional Christian beliefs are eroding. While most people say religion is important to them, they are increasingly likely to feel that "being part of a local church is not a necessity."

Without a strong, clear reason for being, the local church becomes simply another social club ... optional, and available only in my spare time.

Soul winning creates that reason for being. Soul winning is the heart of God. Soul winning is the reason why we are still here, because Christ will not return until our job is done.

According to Matthew 24:14, "And this gospel of the kingdom, shall be preached in all the world for a witness unto all nations and then shall the end come."

God is patiently waiting for the church to get with the program.

American soldiers in the Persian Gulf Crisis carried slogans, which read, "The way home is through Bagdad." They knew that the only way they would be going home was to finish the task by fighting the battle that awaited them in Bagdad.

Christians also must realize that the only way to our heavenly home is through the dark streets of a sin-sick world. The good news is that God has given us everything that we need to win this battle. He's even allowed us to read the last chapter. And we already know that we win!

4) A Consistent, Faithful, Persevering Church

We must walk by faith and not by sight, no matter how long the battle wages or how long the journey becomes. We must believe that the battle is the Lord's.

The children of Israel marched around Jericho a total of thirteen times, never knowing how or when God was going to bring the victory. The victory came, not because of their marching or their shouting, but simply because of their patient obedience.

Jesus spoke a lot about the Last Days, and the disciples were as curious then as we are today. They often asked Jesus to explain and to be clearer about what He meant.

In Matthew 24:3, they came right out and asked Jesus "Tell us, when shall these things be, and what shall be the sign of thy coming, and of the end of the world?"

Jesus answered by speaking about wars and rumors of war and troubled times that the world would see. "For nation shall rise against nation, and kingdom against kingdom: and there shall be famines, and pestilences, and earthquakes, in divers places. All these are the beginning of sorrows" (Matt. 24:7-8).

The word sorrows in the Greek is *odin*, and it means birth pangs, speaking of the pain of childbirth. God's plans and purpose for the Last Days will not come easily, nor will it come without pain. The church without spot or wrinkle, the church of strength and power, will develop as a baby in the womb over a process of time and will come forth through the pain of childbirth.

In the midst of all the confusion in the

world, God intends for His church to come
forth in these Last Days to do the work of
the ministry.

Again, Jesus said in Matthew 24:14,
"And this gospel of the kingdom shall be
preached in all the world for a witness
unto all the nations, and then shall the
end come."

In the midst of it all, we have a job to
do. In the midst of it all, the gospel shall
be preached. This verse reads as a command, it reads as a prerequisite to Christ's
coming. God is waiting for us to complete
our work of preaching the gospel, and then
the end will come.

Indeed, the last words of Jesus before
his ascension into heaven are found in
Mark 16:15, "Go ye into all the world and
preach the gospel to every creature."

The term *go ye*, simply means you go,
speaking to every born-again believer who
carries the name of Christ. Christian, we
have a mission. It's a mission that God
Himself has ordained us to and empow-
ered us for by putting Himself within us.

II Corinthians 3:5-6 says, "Not that we
are sufficient of ourselves to think anything as of ourselves; but our sufficiency is
of God; Who also hath made us able min-

isters of the new testament; not of the letter, but of the spirit: for the letter killeth, but the spirit giveth life."

We are called, commissioned, and equipped.

According to John 15:16, "Ye have not chosen me, but I have chosen you, and ordained you, that ye should go and bring forth fruit, and that your fruit should remain: that whatsoever ye shall ask of the father in my name, he may give it you."

It's time for the church to awake to the true source of her power. It's not in hearing another sermon or reading another book or listening to another set of tapes. Rather, it's acting upon the power and the authority of the Holy Spirit that lives within us. It's time for the church to take her earthly mission seriously and stop being so anxious to go to Heaven.

The story is told about a fiery preacher delivering a sermon about Heaven to an enthusiastic crowd. At a point of emotional crescendo, he pounds the podium and asks the proverbial question, "So how many of you want to go to Heaven."

Everybody's hand shot up except for little Johnny in the front row. Leaning forward as though to capture Johnny's attention, the preacher shouted the question again.

"How many of you want to go to heaven?"

Again all the hands shot up except little Johnny's.

Bewildered, the preacher stopped and directed a question to Johnny. "So, Johnny, don't you want to go to heaven when you die?"

"Yes, sir," exclaimed Johnny, "I want to go there when I die, but I thought you were trying to get up a group to go right now"!

Heaven is our reward, and it is a place that we should think about with great expectation, but not at the expense of doing the job here and now.

The timetable of Christ's return is contingent upon the Church arising to the task of taking the gospel to all the nations. This is the hour when the Church must arise upon the earth as a force to be reckoned with. As Dr. Fuchsia Pickett, seasoned teacher and prophetess, often says, "Before we [the Church] leave, the world is going to know we've been here!"

6.

IT BEGINS WITH LEADERSHIP

Ministry with strong and lasting impact needs proper leadership. Leadership in the local church must come from the pastor. Effective leadership requires true heartfelt vision. Heartfelt vision does not come secondhand. It must come through firsthand experience. This is to say, the pastor must have firsthand experience in local evangelism in order to receive true heartfelt vision for it.

The only way to get a person genuinely interested in overseas missions is to take him to the mission field. I encourage people to go ahead and spend the money that it takes to buy the airline ticket and experience a week or more on the mission field. One could argue that the same money would be better spent buying food to feed the hungry.

The principle holds that you can give a man a fish and feed him for a day, or you can teach him how to fish and feed him for a lifetime. This principle applies to a person interested in the mission field, in that, after he has made the trip personally, he will return with a firsthand vision for what can be accomplished.

In the weeks and years that follow, he will share the vision with others, and directly or indirectly, he will bring far more support to that mission field than what he originally spent on the airline ticket. So how does a local pastor get out into his community and experience the local mission field first hand? I'll tell you what I did.

I accompanied a sheriff's deputy, one of the members of our church, on his night beat of the streets of our city. He invited me to go with him, specifically intending to open my eyes to the realities that existed there. I was shocked at what I saw in our little town. There were prostitutes on the streets and drug dealers, as well as alcoholics and homeless. That evening we visited a couple of adult bookstores and bars, and I discovered another whole world of hurting people. The deputy commented, "Most good people don't realize what is going on in their city after dark, because it happens during the time when they're in their homes and already in bed."

I believe the first step for any leader is to see with his own eyes the needs around him. As Jeremiah states, in Lamentations 3:51, "My eye has affected my heart..."

Our heart can be unaffected by something that we hear second hand or simply read about. However, when you see it first-hand, it gets into your spirit, and the urge to do something about it becomes over-whelming.

Additionally, the needs of every city are a little different. The problems are pretty much the same because people are essentially the same. The way in which different cities address their problems varies sub-stantially.

Often there are government-supported agencies and programs addressing and dealing with some of the problems, but in every case, there is an opportunity for the church to pick-up the loose ends and fill in the cracks.

Our solution is one that deals with the heart of man. Our solution is internal and carries with it supernatural and lasting solutions.

Pastor, let me encourage you to see for yourself. Take somebody that you can trust with you and go spy out the land of your city. Take off your necktie. Dress casually. Go incognito. Get a real look at the community that your church is called of God to reach.

This exercise alone is difficult for most of us, because it goes against our traditional thinking of being separate and "set apart" from the world (II Cor. 6:17). However, further review of the context of these scriptures will reveal that we are to be separate in a spiritual sense and not in a physical one (Phil. 2:15, John 16:33, I John 4:4).

Indeed, the whole purpose of Christ's ministry on earth was to give us an example of how to move toward people and go into every man's world. We are to occupy this world for Christ. We are to go into enemy territory and shine brightly, as a beacon of hope, drawing those with needs toward the brightness of our shining. We are answer vessels for a world riddled with problems.

There is a call in this decade for grass roots evangelism. We must get into the trenches and experience firsthand what we

are instructing and exhorting the body of
Christ to do. They will follow our example.
They will learn on the job. And they will
grow in the process.

The Apostle Paul noted in I Corinthians
4:15, "For though ye have ten thousand
instructors in Christ, yet have ye not many
fathers."

It's easier preached than practiced. A
good father teaches by example. In verses
16, Paul says, "Wherefore I beseech you,
be ye followers of me." The word "followers" in the Greek is *mimetes*, meaning imi-
tators. In Corinthians 11:1, Paul amplifies
the point, "Be ye followers of me, even as
I also am of Christ."

Are we willing to practice what we
preach? Are we willing to put the message
that we believe to the test? Are we willing
to engage the enemy and put the power
of God to the test?

I believe the world is asking those questions of us and all creation cries out for a
deliverer. Jesus made it clear that He has
given us the knowledge and the power to
be that deliverer. Jesus said in Matthew
16:18 that the gates of Hell would not
prevail against the saints.

It's time to occupy. It's time to posses

the land that God has promised. It's time for leadership to set the pace and lead the way!

Street Ministry

Street ministry carries with it a wide variety of definitions, as well as a mixed review of its true effectiveness. We often caculate its value based on the number of souls saved or people fed or help delivered in some measurable way.

I have learned a far greater value derived from personal ministry on the streets. That is, the value of what it does for me personally. I mean, what it does for my spirit, my testimony, and my passion.

Walking through our local shopping mall one day, I witnessed a rare scene. A zealous young man, standing up on a bench, was preaching at the top of his voice about his conversion and the change Jesus had made in his life. Curious and captivated people stopped to watch. The young man had a good word. He drew a crowd and people seemed to listen. That is, until security guards accosted him and roughly led him away.

Nobody there got saved and one could

certainly question the wisdom and effectiveness of that witnessing style. However, the young man was unquestionably gaining confidence, vision, and personal experience from such a bold endeavor. He drew a crowd, and his voice was heard. I had to admire him.

Charles Finney once said, "Get on fire for God and people will come to see you burn!"

Street evangelism has one outstanding advantage. Here is one place where you can always find people with desperate needs. People end up on the streets for a variety of reasons, but they all center around some specific need.

When I refer to "the streets," I'm speaking of that part of your city that is notorious for crime, corruption, sex, or sleazy bars. Evil results when people try to meet their needs in ungodly or illegal ways. Certain areas of the city actually cater to this evil through zoning that permits businesses like topless bars, adult bookstores, and cheap hotel rooms.

The sad truth is that in a godless society, there is a continuous demand for these forms of entertainment. The world generally tolerates them as a viable answer to the needs and cravings of man. And people who don't use the Bible as a standard for their lives will instead use the laws of the land as a guide. They think, "If it's legal, it must be okay."

But these solutions, offered by the world, are temporary fixes at best. The Church has a better solution! The Bible offers an eternal solution. As we get more familiar with the needs, we can learn more perfectly how to apply our solution to the world's needs. Can a Godly solution really be administered on the streets, or must it be administered in the church building itself?

As I ventured out onto the streets of our city, God began to speak more clearly about what to do next. I felt impressed that I should never go alone. Just as Jesus sent out the disciples, two-by-two, this is a good pattern for us when we're moving into enemy territory. A team of two serves not only as a protection, but also as a source of inspiration, wisdom, and account-ability.

Jesus sent the disciples out two-by-two (Mark 6:7, Luke 10:1.) Ecclessiastes 4:12 says, "A three fold cord is not easily bro-ken." That could mean you and me and the Holy Spirit.

Going out on the street alone can be dangerous. Also, I've discovered that "three's a crowd," and tends to scare people off. So, going two-by-two is both biblical and acceptable on the streets.

God also gave me an indication of what to expect in terms of success. I was impressed not to expect anything. In other words, not to go out on the streets expecting to notch my gun with multiple conversions, but rather, to feel successful just by being out there. Just to go and get closer to the needs, in direct obedience to God's Word, would be enough reward.

I felt that God was instructing me to look for the 10 percent that were at a particular crossroad or crisis in their life. I should not expect everyone to be receptive to my words, but look for those who were actually seeking a solution to their crisis; that may only be one in ten.

God promised that He would provide me with divine appointments, opportunities to talk to people that I didn't humanly create. God promised that He would divinely ordain meetings with certain people and opportunities for ministry if we would humbly allow Him to do it.

I began by establishing one night a

week that I could give myself to street ministry. I found a partner who was equally interested in this kind of evangelism, and we began to go out each week, faithfully.

Each night before we went, we would pray and ask God to provide divine appointments. We would confess our own inability to do anything in our own strength and promise not to try to make anything happen. We were simply making ourselves available to talk to everyone that came in our path.

The hour was late. We would go out at 9:00 P.M. and return home anytime from 1:00 to 2:00 in the morning, depending on how much activity we experienced.

We walked the streets, stopping in all the bars along the way, looking for people to talk to, and most people seemed interested in talking. In a bar we would sit down and order a can of soda or a cup of coffee . . . if they served coffee. We would befriend the bartender, play pool, and throw darts and talk to people about everything . . . everything except the Lord . . . waiting for that divine opportunity.

Surprisingly, God would often have them bring up the subject of God, moving our casual conversation into an opportunity to comfortably and effectively share Christ.

In the bars, as much as we tried to blend in, everybody could see that there was something different about us. Obviously, we weren't drinking or smoking or using foul language typical of the bar scene. Of course, every bar has its own personality and clientele, much like the different denominations of our churches. There are biker bars, cowboy bars, sports bars, teen clubs, and the list goes on.

I remember an early experience we had one night, walking into a particularly tough bar. It was the Sunset Tavern, a bikers' bar, known for being bad to the bone.

We strolled in and shoved up to the bar. Immediately the bartender rushed over.

"You must be new in town, fellows," she shouted over the blare of the jukebox.

"No," I returned, "I've lived here about all my life."

"Well then," she said, "You should know that this is a bikers' bar . . . bikers and rednecks."

Her comment was made with a definite "you're out of place here" edge. It

wasn't hard to see that we didn't fit in.
Most of the guys were wearing leather jack-
ets and boots, carrying the symbols and
colors of the bike clubs they rode with.

I looked around and noticed the tough
characters seated on both sides of us. They
were listening intently.

Each situation we encountered on the
streets was different, and we really didn't
plan in advance what we were going to say
or do. We learned to depend upon the
Holy Spirit and respond rather spontaneously.

The bartender was awaiting my response. I looked down the bar and noticed one of the men particularly tuned in
to our conversation.

The next thing I heard come out of my
mouth was, "Well, what category is he in?"
I pointed to the one peering at us.

This comment might have sounded
sarcastic and could have gotten me in
trouble, except that I believe God was directing my lips.

The bartender responded quickly. "Oh,
that's just George," she said, "he's a regular here." Her words became a bit more
friendly, as if to neutralize the situation.

George's eyes locked onto mine. His

firm, weather-beaten face was framed with a reddish beard on his chin and a red bandanna around his forehead.

"I'll play you a game of pool for twenty dollars," he said, tauntingly.

"There'll be no gambling here," the bartender barked. Perhaps she suspected that we could be undercover cops.

"No," I said, returning my attention to George. "I'm not really that good at pool. You'd just be taking my money."

Undaunted, George noted my reluctance and lowered the ante. "How about for ten dollars," he said.

"No," I replied. "Really, I don't want to lose my money."

"Okay," he said. "How about just for fun."

"You're on," I replied, and before I knew it we were racking it up for a game of nine-ball.

The fever was high for pool that night because there was a tournament coming up that weekend. George and I played, surrounded by a crowd of boisterous bikers, and to my chagrin, I almost beat him.

But more importantly, I made a friend. It might be hard on your theology to know that we never talked about the Lord that night, but we earned our welcome for the next visit.

The next time we pushed through the door of the Sunset Tavern, we announced our entry with, "Hey is George here to-night?" Everybody relaxed. We might not look like bikers, but if we knew George . . . we must be okay. A friendship with George meant a welcome in that bar. God knew what He was doing.

For three months my partner and I walked the streets, frequenting bars in our city with little tangible results. But you can be sure that we were learning a lot. God was giving us a feel for the people and a compassion for their needs.

It was an education on the front lines, in the fox holes. It was what I needed to bring passion into my preaching. It was what I needed to discover how desper-ately the world needs Jesus.

The Call of a Leader

There are three kinds of people in the world. Those who make things happen, those who watch things happen, and those who wonder what happened.

A leader is one who is willing to do something before everybody else is doing it. A leader is a step ahead.

I heard Bob Mumford once say, "You get one step ahead of the crowd, and they call you a leader. You get two steps ahead, and they call you a pioneer. You get three steps ahead, and they may be calling you a martyr!"

Actually, spiritual leadership is servanthood. God doesn't make leaders. He makes servants who become leaders. Leadership is not a position, but rather an activity. And it's an activity to which we are all called.

You are saved to serve. You are delivered to be a deliverer.

Moses was the great deliverer of the children of Israel, leading them out of Egypt's slavery. In Exodus 2, we can discover the stages of leadership that he walked through and learn some principles of leadership.

1. Make a grown up decision—Exodus 2:11-14

Like Moses, there comes a time in every man's life where he discovers who he is and what God's plan is for his life. Hebrews 11:24 tells us that Moses chose God over Pharaoh. His spiritual eyes were opened to the injustices and bondages of the people, and he felt compassion.

Proverbs 29:18 says, "Without a vision, the people perish." Moses received vision, supernatural perception, and set out to change things.

However, he wasn't ready. In his zeal and character deficiencies, he ended up killing an Egyptian. Moses needed more preparation. God knew that he needed more patience and love in order to properly do the job he was called to do.

2. Allow time for preparation—Exodus 2:15-24

How long does it take in preparation? Only God knows. Moses was 40-years-old and had already been trained in the best schools of his day. In Pharaoh's palace he learned to read and write. He learned the latest military strategies and governing skills, but it wasn't enough.

God knew he needed some desert experience. He needed some tempering down. Moses had a bad temper, so God knew what he needed to temper down . . . marriage! It's been said, "Love is blind, but marriage is an eye opener!"

For forty more years, Moses shepherded goats in the desert. Then in verse 23, we see things began to happen. The King of

Egypt died, the Israelites groaned in their slavery, and God heard their cry and remembered His promise.

God has a timetable. Sometimes you simply have to wait. You may be doing everything right, but you simply have to wait for other things that God is doing, perhaps in other people. Be willing to wait as a part of God's preparation process.

Noah was 600-years-old when his ministry began. Moses was 80-years-old. Jesus was thirty. So be encouraged. God is doing things more quickly these days.

Galatians 6:9 says, "And let us not be weary in well doing: for in due season we shall reap, if we faint not."

According to Habakkuk 2:3, "For the vision is yet for an appointed time, but at the end it shall speak, and not lie: though it tarry, wait for it; because it will surely come, it will not tarry."

3. Take off your shoes—Exodus 3

A burning bush experience will often mark the end of the season of testing and preparation. I'm speaking of a divine revelation or experience with God. The crisis gets our attention and then God appears.

Moses saw the bush on fire without being consumed, but it wasn't until he turned to further investigate this strange happening that God actually spoke to him from the bush. We must be attentive to what God is doing and saying around us, especially in the time of testing.

The final stage of preparation will always require deeper submission to our master. "Take off your shoes," was the Lord's command.

Hey, if I had heard a voice coming out of a burning bush, I would have been out of my shoes!

In those days, servants didn't wear shoes. God was calling Moses to deeper servanthood. In Exodus 3:5-10, there are four things God said.

1. I am God
2. I have seen the problem
3. I have come down to deliver
4. I'm sending you

Note the last statement. "I am sending you." If God can use an ordinary bush to speak through, He can probably use any person He chooses.

"But God hath chosen the foolish things of the world to confound the wise; and God hath chosen the weak things of the world to confound the things that are mighty" (I Cor. 1:27).

God commanded Moses to go, just as He commands us to go into all the world and preach the gospel. But Moses complained, "Who am I that I should go to Pharaoh and bring the Israelites out of Egypt?"

Proverbs 9:10 says, "The fear (respect) of the Lord is the beginning of wisdom . . ." Until we fear God more than we fear Pharaoh (the world), we will never become a deliverer.

4. Prepare for disappointment—Exodus 4:1-12

"What if they don't believe me, or listen to me?" Moses complained. "What if . . ." That's a common excuse.

Actually, God didn't intend for Pharaoh to listen at all. God gave Moses this miraculous plan while at the same time hardening Pharaoh's heart (Exod. 4:21).

God's ways are not man's ways (Isa. 55:8-9). He has a plan, and sees things from a broader perspective. We must learn to trust our Father. He knows best.

Experience with disappointment and persecution is part of God's plan.

II Timothy 3:12 says, "Yea, and all that will live godly in Christ Jesus shall suffer persecution."

According to Philippians 1:29, "For unto you it is given in the behalf of Christ, not only to believe on him, but also to suffer for his sake."

In II Timothy 2:12 it says, "If we suffer, we shall also reign with him: if we deny him, he also will deny us."

The blessings and persecutions come together.

> And Jesus answered and said, "Verily I say unto you, There is no man that hath left house, or brethren, or sisters, or father, or mother, or wife, or children, or lands, for my sake, and the gospel's, But he shall receive an hundredfold now in this time, houses, and brethren, and sisters, and mothers, and children, and lands, with persecutions; and in the world to come eternal life." (Mark 10:29-30)

Even in my own family experience, I discover that I am drawn closer to my children through their failures and persecutions than through their successes. Think about that.

5. Look for an AARON—Exodus 4:10-16

Moses disputed God's call. He complained about his limited speech abilities and begged God to send someone else.

Perhaps he struggled with a speech impediment, but his reluctance angered God.

Nevertheless, God was gracious to suggest that Moses team up with his brother, Aaron, and God promised to help them both. There is power in agreement.

Matthew 18:19 says, "Again I say unto you, That if two of you shall agree on earth as touching anything that they shall ask, it shall be done for them of my Father which is in heaven."

Ecclesiastes 4:9-10 says, "Two are better than one, because they have a good reward for their labour. For if they fall, the one will lift up his fellow: but woe to him that is alone when he falleth; for he hath not another to help him up."

According to Proverbs 27:17, "Iron sharpeneth iron; so a man sharpeneth the countenance of his friend."

Jesus sent the disciples out two-by-two (Mark 6:7, Luke 10:1), and Deuteronomy 32:30 suggests that "one can chase a thousand and two can put ten thousand to flight."

In Exodus Chapters 5-7, we find Moses and Aaron addressing Pharaoh together. By Chapter 8, Moses is speaking for himself. God grows our leadership through our teaming up with others.

Birth/Death/Rebirth

There is a three-phase progression to leadership vision; the birth phase, the death phase, and the supernatural rebirth phase. Each of these can be illustrated in the leadership call of Moses.

Birth

1. Discover who you are—Exodus 2:11 (People of God)
2. See the cause of God—Exodus 2:11 (Saved to serve)
3. Exercise faith toward the call—Exodus 2:12-15 (Do something)

Death

4. Prepare for failure—Exodus 2:12 (Failure of your ways)
5. Be teachable—Exodus 2:16-22 (Wilderness experiences)
6. Be ready for change—Exodus 2:23-24 (God's timing)

Rebirth

7. Burning bush experience—Exodus 3:2 (Divine revelation)
8. Take off your shoes—Exodus 3:5 (Servanthood)
9. God will be with you—Exodus 3:12 (Supernatural help)

I Corinthians 1:26-27 says, "For ye see your calling, brethren, how that not many wise men after the flesh, not many mighty, not many noble, are called: But God hath chosen the foolish things of the world to confound the wise; and God hath chosen the weak things of the world to confound the things which are mighty."

According to II Peter 1:10, "Wherefore brethren, give diligence to make your calling and election sure: for if ye do these things, ye shall never fall."

7.

GET A VISION, GET A LIFE!

Stop living below your potential! God created you to be alive with dreams and visions that are bigger than you are. He intends to give you creative ideas to act on and the resources to see them through.

Quit focusing on your problems. Big problems can bring big promotions. Look for the gold in the fire. Make lemonade out of that lemon.

Get a vision and you'll get a life!

The Apostle Paul had only words of commendation for the church at Ephesus, for the excellence of their faith and love. Yet he prayed that the eyes of their understanding would be enlightened and that their vision would increase.

> I keep asking that the God of our Lord Jesus Christ, the glorious Fa-

> ther, may give you the Spirit of wis-
> dom and revelation, so that you may
> know him better. I pray also that the
> eyes of your heart may be enlight-
> ened in order that you may know the
> hope to which he has called you, the
> riches of his glorious inheritance in
> the saints, and his incomparably great
> power for us who believe. (Eph.
> 1:17-19 NIV)

Get a revelation of God's power at work
in you! In Genesis 37:5, God gave Joseph
a dream about his future and his potential. Joseph held on to the dream. He spoke
of it and focused on it, despite the oppo-
sition and obstacles.

Glance at your problems, but live for
your dreams. God speaks through dreams.
He put those desires in your heart.

Joel 2:28 and Acts 2:17 prophecy that
in the last days, "Your young men shall
see visions, and your old men shall dream
dreams."

Habakkuk 2:2 exhorts us, "Write the
vision, and make it plain upon tables, that
he may run that readeth it."

Proverbs 29:18 simply says, "Where
there is no vision, the people perish. . . . "

Vision can be defined as supernatural

perspective, being able to see beyond the natural and into the supernatural, able to see with the eyes of faith.

Evolution of a Vision

Vision is creative. Vision attracts resources. When God puts something unseen in your spirit, it has the potential of creating awesome things in the natural.

When you receive a vision to do something great for God, you may have no earthly means to accomplish it . . . at least not right away. But, if you begin to speak of the vision, telling others what's in your heart, and allowing it to develop further, then the vision will grow, and others will join you in the vision. Some will work along side you; others will contribute necessary funds, materials, facilities, or other resources.

Faith demands that you step out and speak about what's in your heart. This gives God something to work with.

When God called our family to build a Christian Retreat Center, we had no money of our own with which to begin. As we spoke of the vision, friends and family joined us to begin clearing the land. As a boy, I joined in with my little hatchet, chopping down brush and making room for future roads and buildings. We had sketches of future buildings drawn up. ("And the Lord answered me, and said, Write the vision, and make it plain upon tables, that he may run that readeth it." Hab. 2:2) People started donating money to start construction, and history was being created.

The vision will grow, and the resources will grow.

Now . . . watch out! Earthly resources create a terrible distraction to the supernatural, God-given vision. This is the danger that lurks in the process, aborting many great visions prematurely. Vision is spirit. Resources represent flesh. You must keep your focus on the vision, giving honor and leadership to God for what He has birthed and is directing.

All too often, we get an idea, we get excited, and say, "Thank you God, now I can take it from here!" And He lets us take it . . . by ourselves, to a miserable end.

In Acts 6:2-4, the disciples recognized that the growth of the Church was bringing a dangerous administrative distraction to their time, attention to the Word, and prayer, so they wisely appointed others to those tasks and distanced themselves.

> So the twelve gathered all the disciples together and said, "It would not be right for us to neglect the ministry of the word of God in order to wait on tables. Brothers, choose seven men from among you who are known to be full of the Spirit and wisdom. We will turn this responsibility over to them and will give our attention to prayer and the ministry of the word." (NIV)

Keep your focus on the vision . . . that's spirit. If the ministry mechanics distract you from the vision, the life will soon disappear, and your vision erodes into an institution. It may be a well-funded institution, but the life is gone. This is a picture of some of our traditional denominations today. Many are high on order and administration but low on divine administration.

I've developed a graph (located on page 153) to illustrate this evolution process. The dotted line illustrates that the vision must always continue to grow. We must keep our focus on the the vision through prayer and revelation from God, and then, vision attracts resources.

Evolution of a Vision

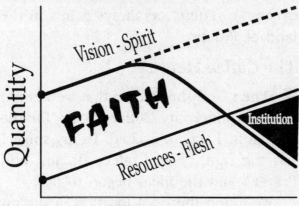

NOTE: You will never have enough resources (money, people, equipment, and facilities) to accomplish the vision that God continues to give, because the vision will always keep growing ahead of the available resources.

But here's the key: The difference between the vision line and the resources line is faith! And remember, "Without faith it's impossible to please God" (Heb. 11:6). God is interested in seeing our faith develop and work to His glory.

God is giving His Church supernatural visions and creative ideas for soul winning in these last days. The Holy Spirit is creative, and He is giving us fresh ideas that will capture the attention of the world.

Yet, there will always be obstacles to overcome. There are always giants in the land of Promise.

The Coffee House

When God showed me that we were to open an inner city Coffee House for the homeless, I was so excited. In my spirit I saw the sign, "Free Coffee, Donuts, and Prayer," and the ideas began to flow.

We found the right location in the inner city. We carefully drew up our plans and took the proposal to City Hall for approval. I presented our ideas with conviction and enthusiasm, confident that city officials would applaud our efforts to help the homeless."

"No, Rev. Derstine, we don't want your Coffee House."

I couldn't believe my ears and asked for clarification. "You mean you want to take it under further advisement? You want us to present the proposal at another hearing?" I stammered.

"No, Rev. Derstine, we don't want your Coffee House."

The disapproval was reiterated in no uncertain terms. There was no need for further discussion or consideration.

I couldn't believe my ears. We had just offered the city a creative approach to solving the homeless problem in our community, backed by all the resources and enthusiasm of our church, and they were saying "no."

Walking down the long tier of steps from City Hall, I complained to God. "I thought you wanted me to start a Coffee House, but they've said no."

"*I* didn't say no!" God responded gingerly.

The lights flickered back on in my spirit. We went back to the drawing board, developing our ideas further, acquiring a lease on the building, and lining up the man power. It took six months of red tape, public hearings, and community debates.

Day after day, week after week, we were front page in our local newspaper, but the coffee house opened!

It was a God idea. The following year we were listed as one of the top-10 newsmakers in our community, celebrated for our innovative programs to help the homeless. We even received commendations from the Mayor and the Keys to the City.

Romans 8:37 says, "In all these things

we are more than conquerors through him that loved us."

According to Psalms 2:1 (TLB), "What fools the nations are to rage against the Lord! How strange that men should try to outwit God!"

Don't just dream. That happens when you sleep. Pursue the prize!

Philippians 3:14 (NIV) says, "I press on toward the goal to win the prize for which God has called me heavenward in Christ Jesus."

Heritage Day Parade

Getting into our local Heritage Day Parade was a God idea, but it didn't happen without obstacles. This event boasts of over one hundred thousand in attendance. It's the biggest annual event in our town, and it wasn't open to church entries.

Our first application was administratively denied by the Parade Marshall. Then God put something in my spirit. Our vision was too small. We needed a grander entry. We needed to bring something of value to the parade.

We redressed ourselves and resubmitted our application, promising to bring an element of family value to this event that had increasingly become a big beer party. Our entry was accepted, this time featuring three floats, live music, dance teams, tambourine teams, and a parade of flags and banners. With over one hundred participants, our entry continues to be the largest in the entire parade. A powerful witness for Christ. A God idea!

Caroling in the Bars

On Christmas Eve, we organize teams of carolers and go bar-hopping. Every open bar in town is targeted. Each caroling team is made up of eight to ten people and at least one musical instrument (guitar, accordion, trumpet, violins). Instruments give the groups more credibility.

I'll walk through the door with an accordion slung over my shoulder. "Anyone up for some good Christmas music?" I'll announce loudly and gregariously, looking for an affirmative response. Usually we're readily and warmly received. They're surprised that we're there . . . but appreciative.

Our carolers hold lighted candles to create atmosphere, and patrons are encouraged to sing along. Then we hand out gifts of little red Bibles wrapped in Christmas paper with a small candy cane attached. We engage in conversation with the intention of praying for every person in the place, one-on-one. It's a fruitful and rewarding ministry that can be effective in any town. A God idea.

Incidentally, don't expect all churches or churched people to understand or appreciate your ministry in the bars. We've been conditioned to stay away from the world, to a fault. I've had pastors publicly denounce our unconventional evangelism efforts and warn their people to stay away.

Admittedly, the bars are not for everyone, especially anyone with an alcohol addiction problem, but they are places that desperately need the Light of Christ.

Karaoke

If you're a singer, God may anoint you to sing Karaoke in a bar. Karaoke sound tracks are provided in some bars to give customers platform to sing along with their favorite tunes.

My partner and I took the platform one night in a bar to sing a Karaoke version of Amazing Grace, all four verses. I took the opportunity to introduce the song and share personal testimony. The anointing of God swept in, and people were visibly moved. When we finished singing, many came up to us in tears, expressing their feelings and requesting prayer. It seemed like an altar call in the middle of the bar.

When you're operating in vision, you are fearless. Your commitment to the cause of Christ overcomes your natural inhibitions. You're operating under the anointing of God.

It was the boldness of the disciples that impressed the crowd in Acts 4:13. "Now when they saw the boldness of Peter and John and perceived that they were unlearned and ignorant men, they marvelled; and they took knowledge of them, that they had been with Jesus."

I'm sold on being bold!

Your boldness will carry your testimony for God. Be willing to stand out in the crowd. Be willing to get some media attention.

Harnessing the Media

When you're out there doing something, you can expect to get noticed. You will become newsworthy. That's good. In order to get our message out to the masses, we must capture mass media attention.

Traditionally the church has shied away from secular media attention for fear of being misrepresented or misquoted. It's time for the church to take her rightful place among the movers and shapers of our world. Our message must be heard. We must take the risk of being misunderstood.

As we learn how the media world works, we can learn how to harness this powerful tool to advance our cause.

Jesus said, in Matthew 10:16, "Behold, I send you forth as sheep in the midst of wolves: be ye therefore wise as serpents, and harmless as doves."

What Is News?

News is a business. Its product is the timely report of events, facts, and opinions that interest a significant number of people. News reporters gather and publish information that interests people, information that others will buy.

Elements of Newsworthiness

Learn how to make your event newsworthy, and you can tap into a wealth of free publicity. Here are some of the elements of newsworthiness.

1. Conflict—Is there a conflict? Con-

flict creates interest. Conflict is dramatic, it's emotional, and it can lead to change. There's always two sides to a story. Reporters intentionally look for opposing views.

Our first year of Hell House exploded into the public eye through concern over the size and offensiveness of our sign.

City officials wanted us to remove the word "Hell" from the storefront window, or at least make it smaller. I called the press and capitalized on the debate, and we made the front page of our local paper for days running. The free publicity drew thousands of teens to our event. We couldn't have bought that kind of advertising.

2. Unusualness—Here we're talking of firsts, record-setting events or uniqueness. Can you add something to your event that will make it more unusual?

After we had been feeding the homeless a meal in the park each week for a few years, the press lost interest, and we were out of the news for a while. To reignite media interest, we invited a group of children from a home for the mentally challenged, and they assisted us in serving the food one night. It made the event newsworthy, and reporters came out to cover the story.

3. Local interest—It's considered that 85 percent of newspaper readers are primarily interested in news of local consequence or in close proximity (my property or my neighborhood). Keep your local papers aware of your church events that are of community interest.

When we bring in a foreign pastor or missionary, especially from a country that is presently in the news, our local media are interested. It's important that we understand their angle of interest, so that we can present the event as an opportunity to inform an interested public.

4. Human interests—People like hearing about other interesting people. You can get personal profiles or success stories written up about the people working with you, or the people you've helped.

We had a family of circus performers in our church who worked with the Ringling Brothers Barnum and Bailey Circus. They sometimes performed at our street outreaches, helping to draw a crowd. Their participation always drew interests from local reporters.

5. Prominence—Add a political figure, professional athlete, or public celebrity to your event, and it immediately becomes

newsworthy. We've had people of national prominence, like Oliver North, Cal Thomas, Rosie Grier, Richard Kiel (Jaws), and Pat Boone, to name a few. But even local government, law enforcement, or school officials will draw media attention.

Handling Reporters

1. Prepare yourself in advance, if possible, to give the facts . . . who, what, where, why, and how?

2. Consider lead lines, quips, quotes and anecdotes. It helps reporters write their stories and can help insure an accurate message. Remember, they're on a tight publication schedule and need all the help they can get.

3. When you're dealing with sensitive issues or when you don't want to give exhaustive answers, use written, prepared statements. A carefully prepared statement is usually better than a "no comment."

4. Be courteous. Be human. Be yourself. Remember, they're human, too, and will respond to your feelings and emotions.

5. Keep eye contact and be aware of your nonverbal communication. They will report on their observations and impres-

sions as well as what you have to say.

6. Be brief. Get to the point. Less is best. Sometimes they'll let you talk on and on and simply extract the story they already have in mind.

7. Consider whether they are writing a news story or a feature story. News tends to stick to the facts without hidden agenda. A feature story, on the other hand, is intended to entertain and can carry a lot more color. . . sensation, humor, or skepticism. Of course, no reporting is totally objective or without bias.

8. Give credit where credit is due. If they write a good article, call and commend them. Also, hold them accountable for unfair reporting. Let them know you've read the report.

9. Develop relationships. Reporters are often thick-skinned. They're used to taking their punches. Your efforts toward friendship will be appreciated.

10. Let church leadership or a designated spokesman speak for the church. Instruct the staff and congregation on this point as well. Reporters use quotes to validate their stories, often comparing testimony. People on your staff or in the church talking out of turn can breech relationships and confuse the truth.

Publicity Sources

Explore the variety of ways that are available for getting your message out. The Gospel must be preached and published. There are many avenues of communication that cost little or nothing except your time and effort. Here are some to consider.

1. Paid advertising—Newspaper, magazines, television, radio, mailing lists. This can get very expensive. Negotiate.

2. Public Service Announcements and News Releases.

3. Community Calendars, Bulletin Boards, Listings.

4. News Stories.

5. Editorials—These come by request of the publisher.

6. Letters to Editor—These are your submissions, perhaps in response to other letters or current news issues.

7. Brochures, Flyers, Posters.

8. Direct Mail, Newsletters, Church Bulletins.

9. Door-to-Door Handouts, Door Hangers.

10. Telephone, FAX, E-Mail, Internet.

8.

THE JESUS WAY

In Matthew 4:19, Jesus said, "Follow me, and I will make you fishers of men."

Follow me! Follow my example. Do as I do. Do it My way!

Jesus seemed to understand that we would need to study His example. He knew that it would require a learning process as he said, "... and I will *make* you."

It's even clearer in Mark's account of this scripture.

"And Jesus said unto them, Come ye after me, and I will make you to become fishers of men" (Mark 1:17).

When Jesus originally said these words, He was talking to men who already were fishers of fish. But He said, "I will make you to become fishers of men." They may have known a lot about fishing for fish, but they needed to follow Jesus in order to learn how to fish for men.

It's significant that Jesus related the work of soul winning to that of fishing, not aerospace engineering! Fishing isn't glamorous. Fishing isn't pretty. But it's something everybody can understand.

Some people must think soul winning is like the work of an attorney because they try to build a case for the Gospel and try to debate people into salvation.

Others see it more from an accountant's perspective, balancing the accounts and showing people where they come up short.

But Jesus rounded up a few scruffy, unrefined fishermen, a little rough around the edges, and said, "Let me show you that anyone can do this stuff!" (My words)

Maybe He also chose fishing because it is something you have to *go* do. When He said, "Go ye," He meant that you can't expect to harvest the fields or catch a fish from the church pew. You'll have to go.

Hook, Line, and Sinker

One time I was out fishing with a rusty old Zebco 101 rod and reel. In the excitement of catching the big one, my reel jammed up. I panicked and grabbed the end of the rod, and it snapped. Desperately, I began drawing the line in with my hands . . . and I heard the voice of God say, "All you really need is a hook, line, and sinker."

Jesus is the hook. He is the Way, the Truth, and the Life. His work on the cross is the barb that keeps people hooked on.

The Word is the line. It keeps us rightly connected to God. Some people talk a good line, but their words are powerless without God's Word.

The sinker performs an important function. It gets the bait off the surface and down to where the fish are. The sinker is your testimony. It's what transforms the letter of the Word into spirit and life. People want to know how God has made a difference in your life and how He can be relevant to theirs.

Of course, you are the bait. The thing you must ask yourself is, are you live bait or dead bait? I've always found live bait works better. Then there are those who act like cut bait, they're always murmuring or complaining about something.

Our lives are to be "living epistles" read of all men (II Cor. 3:2). Your testimony can be your strongest tool to draw people to the gospel. From there you simply need to open your mouth, and God will fill it with the right words to speak.

"But I'm afraid," You might think. So was the Apostle Paul! In I Corinthians 2:3 (NIV), he says, "I came to you in weakness and fear, and with much trembling."

Then Paul reveals the true source of his strength.

> Brothers, think of what you were when you were called. Not many of you were wise by human standards; not many were influential; not many were of noble birth. But God chose the foolish things of the world to shame the wise; God chose the weak things of the world to shame the strong. He chose the lowly things of this world and the despised things— and the things that are not—to nullify the things that are, so that no one may boast before Him. (I Cor. 1:26-29 NIV)

"But he said to me, 'My grace is sufficient for you, for my power is made perfect in weakness.' Therefore I will boast all the more gladly about my weaknesses, so that Christ's power may rest on me" (II Cor. 12:9 NIV).

Our adversary, the devil, has tried to convince God's people that we should be afraid to witness. He has suggested that the world will reject our testimony. That isn't true. Not today.

One Christmas Eve, when we were caroling in the bars, my group was largely made up of "first-time out" soul winners. We were on our way into a particularly rough cowboy bar, called the Southern Comfort Saloon. I decided to begin with a lighter song on our repertoire, "Jingle Bells," inviting all to sing-a-long with us. A rough character at a table in the front shouted out, "Come on, sing about Jesus! We know why you're here!"

It was a little unnerving.

After we sang our list of songs, I sat down at his table to talk. "You're not afraid of us, are you?" he barked, more like a statement than a question. Then he said something I'll never forget, "I'll tell you what, the people in here are more afraid of YOU!"

It's true! The world is waiting for us to be bold enough to share the Truth that we have experienced. They are more afraid of us than we are of them. We have nothing to fear; our hearts have been enlightened. They are still living in darkness and fear and need the light of the gospel!

Jesus said, "Follow me, and I will make
you fishers of men." Follow Jesus to where
the fish are . . . to the streets and bars, to
the hospitals, nursing homes, schools, jails,
and penitentiaries. Go to the racetrack,
motorcycle rallies, rodeos, fairs, parades . . .
everywhere that people gather.

The "What Would Jesus Do?" (WWJD)
expression is more than a clever phrase. It
is our marching orders.

He is our example and hero, not
Michael Jordan or Madonna. His word is
our textbook and training manual, not *Teen
Magazine* or *GQ*. His approval is our desire, not human peer pressure. His promise is our reward, not the wealth or riches
of this world.

When the WWJD bracelets came out, I
put one on and never took it off. I wear it
as a covenant bracelet with God, much
like my wedding ring signifies a covenant
with my wife. It reminds me of my vows
and of God's promises. It reminds me that
God's agenda is more important than my
own.

Remember the pattern for sharing the
Gospel, the Jesus way. Get it into your
spirit. Get interested in the Father's business. Here is the pattern for review.

1. Smile—Create an atmosphere of kindness & acceptance.

2. Engage in conversation—Jesus moved toward people (Matt. 14:14, Mark 6:34), so must we. Be outspoken. Take an active interest in others.

3. Discover their need—You don't have to talk to someone long before they will complain about something. Their need creates an opportunity for prayer.

4. Offer prayer—Consider prayer your highest order of spiritual business, rather than making a convert. Take them by the hand. Expect the windows of heaven to open as you pray. Allow God to intervene by His Spirit.

5. Use discernment—After prayer, pause briefly to observe what God is doing. You may see tears or receive a request for additional prayer.

6. Introduce Christ—Ask them if they want an assurance of salvation and the promise of eternal life. Lead them through a "Believer's Prayer."

7. Make an appointment—Never leave a new Believer without a follow-up appointment, perhaps to bring them to church. Satan will try to steal the Word as soon as you leave. They will stand stronger if they

know when they will see you again.

Jesus said, "Go ye into all the world and preach the gospel." It means you go. To obey is better than sacrifice (I Sam. 15:2). Partial obedience is disobedience. Make a decision, step out, and be counted.

Matthew 7:21 is a grave word; "Not every one that saith unto me Lord, Lord, shall enter into the kingdom of heaven; but he that doeth the will of my Father which is in heaven."

He that does the will of God.

Hebrews 5:8 tells us that Jesus, ". . . became the author of eternal salvation unto all them that obey him."

Where do you stand today? Are you about the Father's business? Or will you come up lacking on the day of His return?

Covenant Prayer

Join me now in a covenant prayer of obedience to Christ's command. Purpose in your heart that you will not live life's business as usual in these critical Last Days. Get prepared to engage the enemy and join the ranks of God's faithful servants, ready to do His will.

Pray with me.

Dear Jesus. Thank you for your saving grace and life changing power at work in me now. I put my faith in your Word and covenant today to walk in obedience to your command; to go into all the world and preach the gospel, to look for the opportunities that you bring to my path and boldly open my mouth to give testimony, offer prayer, and minister by unction of your Spirit. I purpose to make soul winning a top priority in my life because it is your top priority. I yield my body, soul, and spirit to your divine purpose, and I put away everything that is displeasing to you. Help me Lord in my pursuit of holiness, and hear my prayers in the quiet place. For you oh Lord are my hope, my strength, and my eternal destiny. Amen.